Crossover Comments

Kingdom Blessings,

2 Chronicles 20:20 says something very powerful that we can't afford to miss. It says, "Believe in the words of the Prophets and you shall prosper."

Well, there is a Prophetic Voice in the land arising in the person of Prophet D. John Coleman. In his latest book, "Crossover - Better is on the Other Side," he presents an exposé on the journey of the people of God in the Old Testament from Egypt to the Promised Place.

Prophet Coleman does an excellent job of juxtaposing their journey then and our spiritual journey now. All of us face crossovers from poverty to prosperity, from burdens to blessings, from anger to His anointing.

Whether you are looking for a crossover in the natural or spiritual, this book is a must-read for your journey.

~ Apostle H. Daniel Wilson,
Valley Kingdom Ministries International, Oak Forest, IL

In his new book, Prophet D. John Coleman delivers a clear prophetic call for all readers to come up and out of their circumstances into their God-designed purpose. I found this book extremely practical, with useful steps lighted with Scripture for an easy pathway to follow in order to Crossover into my NEXT.

~ Bishop Walter Harvey, Apostle - Embassy Center, Milwaukee, WI; Executive Presbyter - Assemblies of God

As we find ourselves at the "head of the year" (Rosh Hashanah), Crossover is the perfect book to start your year off with a Holy Ghost bang! It is filled with quotes, erudite advice, strategies, and Scriptural underpinnings to assist you in getting to your "better," which resides directly on the other side of your difficult situations.

In his latest literary endeavor, Coleman expertly navigates and illuminates the many satanic obstacles that attempt to prevent or hinder your success in God! He equips the reader with the liberty of clarity, teaches how to break the Spirit of Pharaoh, provides seven ways to maximize every moment of the day, offers decrees and declarations, and much, much more! I truly believe that this book will bless you in more ways than one. Get your copy today!

~ John Veal, Author of the books, "Supernaturally Prophetic" and "Supernaturally Delivered"

Crossover is without a doubt one of the best reads I've encountered all year. Prophet D. John Coleman walks the reader through the process of discovering their destiny, their God-given talents, and their gifts. Once you've finished reading this work of art, you will agree that better is on the other side.

~ Bishop Alvernis Johnson, Kingdom Life Ministries, Saginaw, MI

CROSSOVER
—Better Is on the Other Side—

D. John Coleman

DELAND JOHN COLEMAN
MINISTRIES

In Conjunction with

"Crossover – Better Is on the Other Side"

by D. John Coleman

Some Scripture references may be paraphrased versions or illustrative references of the author. All Scripture quotations are taken from the KJV, Amplified, The Passion Translation, New Living Translation, The Message, and New International Version of the Holy Bible, unless otherwise noted.

New International Version (NIV)

Scripture quotations marked (NIV) are taken from the Holy Bible, New International Version®, NIV®. Copyright © 1973, 1978, 1984 by Biblica, Inc.™

The Holy Bible: English Standard Version (ESV)

Scripture quotations marked "ESV" are from the ESV Bible® (The Holy Bible, English Standard Version®). Copyright © 2001 by Crossway Bibles, a publishing ministry of Good News Publishers.

Amplified Bible (AMP)

Copyright © 2015 by The Lockman Foundation, La Habra, CA 90631. All rights reserved.

King James Version (KJV) Public Domain

The New Living Translation (NLT) is an English translation of the Bible. The origin of the NLT came from a project aiming to revise The Living Bible (TLB). This effort eventually led to the creation of the NLT—a new translation separate from the TLB. The NLT relies on critical editions of the original Hebrew and Greek texts. The first NLT edition (published in 1996) retains some stylistic influences of the TLB, but these are less evident in text revisions that have been published since.

The Message: The Bible in Contemporary Language (MSG) is a version of the Bible by Eugene H. Peterson published in segments from 1993 to 2002.

The Passion Translation (TPT)

Scripture quotations marked TPT are from The Passion Translation®. Copyright © 2017, 2018, 2020 by Passion & Fire Ministries, Inc. Used by permission. All rights reserved. ThePassionTranslation.com. Published by BroadStreet Publishing and translated by Brain Simmons. First released as a New Testament in 2017, The Passion Translation includes additions that do not appear in the source manuscripts, phrases meant to draw out God's "tone" and "heart" in each passage.

References and resources:

- *Bsfinternational.org*
- *Bible-history.com*
- *Notablebiographies.com*
- *Biblestudytools.com*

Cover design, editing, book layout, and publishing services by KishKnows, Inc., Richton Park, Illinois, 708-252-DOIT admin@kishknows.com, www.kishknows.com

ISBN 979-8-218-08842-2

LCCN 2022919184

All rights reserved. No part of this book may be reproduced, distributed, or transmitted in any form or by any means, including photocopying, recording, digital scanning, or other electronic or mechanical methods, without the prior written permission of the publisher, except in the case of brief quotations embodied in critical reviews and certain other non-commercial uses permitted by copyright law. For permission requests, please contact D. John Coleman.

Copyright © 2022 by D. John Coleman.

Printed in the United States of America

Dedication

I would like to dedicate this book to my amazing wife of twenty-six years, Kisia Coleman. You have been faithful and consistent in my life, and I honor you for that!

Acknowledgments

For every believer who has been faced with some type of major opposition, if God can deliver Moses and the children of Israel, He can do the same for you, wherever you are! God is not a respecter of persons; He respects and honors His principles. So, to everyone that grabs a copy of this book, you can make it! You can and will cross over, in Jesus' name.

Table of Contents

Scripture.. *xvi*

Foreword.. *xvii*

Prologue.. *xxi*

"The Comfort Zone"   *1*

Chapter 1

    Things to Avoid if You Want to Succeed.....................   3

        Lack of Discernment..   3

        Carelessness..   6

        Ignorance..   7

        Abuse/Misuse...   8

        Hindered by Tests and Trials........................   10

Chapter 2

    Perspectives of Comfort...................................   15

    The Life of Moses..   19

    The Exodus Moment.......................................   23

Chapter 3

    Qualities of a Leader.. **31**

    Characteristics of a Leader.. **36**

Chapter 4

    The Power of Sacrificing... **45**

    Abraham's Test.. **46**

    Battle of Wills... **50**

Chapter 5

    Pharaoh Will Not Follow You into Your Future!...... **57**

Chapter 6

    Prophetic Word.. **63**

Chapter 7

    Library of Boldness that Breaks the Comfort Zone. **67**

"The Confusion"   **71**

Chapter 8

    Tactics of the Enemy... **73**

    Reclaim and Renew... **77**

    Still Small Voice... **86**

Chapter 9

    A Mephibosheth Moment... **91**

"The Conduct" — 95

Chapter 10
- The Code 97
- Position Affects Conduct 101

Chapter 11
- The Battle between the Soul and the Spirit 103
- Discipline and Diligence 107

Chapter 12
- Library of Conduct 109

"The Clear Vision" — 113

Chapter 13
- Having Clarity 115
- Walking Through that Wilderness 120

Chapter 14
- Arise from the Juniper Tree 123

Chapter 15
- Library of Clarity 131

"The Crossover" — 137

Chapter 16
- Promised Land 139
- Promised Plan 145

Chapter 17

    Breaking the Spirit of Pharaoh.................................... **149**

    Characteristics of the Spirit of Pharaoh..................... **153**

    Holy, Acceptable... **159**

    A Type and Foreshadow.. **163**

Chapter 18

    Prayer for Authority.. **169**

    Be Alert!... **171**

Chapter 19

    His Weight in the Wind... **173**

    Lean on Me.. **178**

    Favorable Conditions.. **179**

Chapter 20

    His Strong Hand... **183**

    He Knows, He Cares.. **187**

    Believe It, and Receive It... **191**

    What to Look For... **198**

Chapter 21

    Prophecy... **201**

    Concluding Remarks... **203**

"The Continuation"   **207**

7 Ways to Maximize Every Moment of the Day This Year.. 209

52 Declarations That Will Defeat Being Dormant.. 213

Author Biography.. 221
Author Contact Information..................................... 224

*"I tell you the truth, whoever hears my word and believes him who sent me has eternal life and will not be condemned; he has CROSSED OVER from death to life." ~ **John 5:24 (NIV)***

Foreword

"Being bold will cost you your convenience."

We really pray that you will discover that you have a destiny in God and that your gift and who you are matters to the Father. The truth is, we all have been hit by some kind of tragedy or storm. I just believe right now that your reading this is not by happenstance; but rather, you're on the mind of God in a major way in this season. God has begun to show me that something massive is about to happen in the Body of Christ this year—and if you're reading this, it's because perhaps, you have a key role in this as well. So, man of God, woman of God, let's clean off our lens in a sense. Let's readjust and focus.

I have personally found that the antidote for distraction or distorted vision is consistently staying focused. Let's be cognizant and attentive to those we give ear to and those who voice their opinions in our lives. Just because someone professes to be your friend does not authorize them or give them special access to speak into your life. However, real spiritual fathers and mothers can speak to real spiritual sons and daughters in the Lord without kickback, resentment, or resistance. When there is a real connection through relationship and covenant-ship, you are able to handle the process of correction and direction. It is so imperative that we all have the individuals that will critique us and cancel whatever may be futile in our developmental process and that we are okay with it.

Whenever you anticipate becoming something great or establishing who you were called to be, it will always require a level of inconvenience. This is something we will experience on a consistent basis and not just when we feel like it. Think about this. For every person that has made an impact or imprint in the world, it has always cost them their convenience. When you consider people from biblical times, such as: Moses, Joseph, Joshua, Samuel, David, and so many others, all of them were willing to take a bold step of faith. Being bold will not always guarantee you that people will be there for you; but if God was there for Moses, so will He be there for you as well.

If you say you're ready to be great but not willing to allow disturbance in you and simply remain dormant, then in actuality, all you're doing is what so many others do at the end of the day; and that is, to accept complacency. When you are really ready, you will eliminate all the excuses that are keeping you from the exceptional.

I heard Apostle Ron Carpenter say, "Until the desire is greater to be set free than that which you're dealing with, you will either choose freedom or be bound indefinitely." Allow the sense of urgency to ignite, and you will give birth to something that you could've only imagined.

So many people haven't gotten that sense of urgency yet, but I pray that the fire of the Holy Spirit will push you out of the room of 'convenience' and into the room where lives are drastically changed by your willingness to step out of your comfort zone.

The exceptional way of living is not automatic. You starting a business is not automatic. A ministry is not automatic nor is writing a book or starting anything that will cost you. The reality is that not everyone is real or authentic. There are some artificial and even fraudulent people out there. They are the kind of people that lurk and prey on the depressed and discouraged all of the time. It's unfortunate, but that's the world we live in, and even the state of church culture to some extent. Something is very wrong when, even in the church, we have a predator spirit that is lusting and manipulating others for their own benefit and advancement.

I get it. Some people are afraid to step out because there are trust issues that may have come from both sides of the spectrum. Because of this, many people don't often trust others that easily.

Just learn this principle: Inspect everything and assume nothing. Inspect what you expect! Learn the difference, and you won't abort your destiny. Remember, people will always have something to say whether good or bad, so you just make sure you keep moving.

I declare that you are about to embark on something that's going to blow your mind and set you up for life! We will discover in this book that every "crossover moment" into a promise will always be preceded by an instruction.

"If you can't fly, then run. If you can't run, then walk. If you can't walk, then crawl; but whatever you do, you have to keep moving forward."
- Martin Luther King, Jr.

Prologue

In this book, we're going to discover how, in life, there are often several things that are related to crossing over to the other side for a better life. You can't just wish for it to happen; you have to plan for it to happen. So, join me as we take a journey into these subjects that I believe will cause you to have an epic life in God. We will be discussing the Comfort Zone, the Confusion, the Conduct, having Clarity, and lastly, the Crossover.

1 Corinthians 15:33-34 NIV

Do not be misled: "Bad company corrupts good character." Come back to your senses as you ought, and stop sinning; for there are some who are ignorant of God—I say this to your shame.

Isaiah 28:23 NIV

Listen and hear my voice; pay attention and hear what I say.

Isaiah 30:20-21 NIV

Although the Lord gives you the bread of adversity and the water of affliction, your teachers will be hidden no more; with your own eyes you will see them. Whether you turn to the right or to the left, your ears will hear a voice behind you, saying, "This is the way; walk in it."

We will see through the life of Moses, the prophet of God, that you may often struggle with your identity and purpose. You may be struggling with things of the past or perhaps dealing with spirits that are like principalities over a region or city. However, with God on your side, you can cross over this Red Sea experience. We have faith in you, and so does your Heavenly Father. Just go ahead, and do it! Let's go together, and dive in!

"Do one thing every day that scares you."

- Eleanor Roosevelt

"THE COMFORT ZONE"

"If you don't want to be uncomfortable, please don't go after success! It will cost you your past and present mindset; but if you do pursue success, it will position you for the best future!"

Chapter 1

THINGS TO AVOID IF YOU WANT TO SUCCEED

Now, let's just jump right into this. Allow me to share a short list of five things that I sense you will need to avoid if you intend to succeed in life, leadership, business, ministry, or just in general, as it relates to your assignment.

Lack of Discernment

What is Discernment?

"Discernment is the ladder that elevates your application and understanding. It is the wheel that causes one to arrive at an intended destination in God. It does not derail because of road blocks and hiccups. It's the microscopic lens we need to see with, in order to steer us in the right direction."

Discernment is defined, in the modern secular sense by Dictionary.com as "the faculty of discerning; discrimination; acuteness of judgment, and understanding". Fundamentally, discernment is the ability to judge well. Whether it's the choices we make or the people we interact with, discernment is the gift of recognizing the moral and practical consequences of our decisions.

Discernment has historically been praised as a valuable trait, allowing those who possess it to avoid costly mistakes or misfortunes.

Furthermore, discernment was primarily a biblical doctrine, occurring in the collection of the gifts of the Holy Spirit as the "Gift of Discerning Spirits"—the gift to recognize whether or not something is truly from God or in accordance with righteousness.

This is one word in the Body of Christ at large that we all need to become more acclimated with. It can assist us in determining the timing or the season of the Lord for our lives corporately or individually. Just taking that additional moment to ponder and consider—to inquire of the Lord—can really make a world of difference.

To some degree, we have all been guilty of only permitting

ourselves to go so far… and then, out of nowhere, we run out of gas, lose motivation, or simply just throw in the towel mentally before we can even pick it back up. Many Christians stop at many different locations in life, and some never really arrive at their desired location. So many people have already quit in their minds by focusing on natural circumstances. We must learn how to overcome the battle in the mind to win in every area of life. I believe this has always been His plan for our lives… for us to be victorious.

As believers, we must be assured of the fact that God is always faithful. We may not be, at times, when it comes to our purpose and pursuit of Him. However, He is always watching out for us in more ways than you and I can fathom.

Let's not allow situations in life to cause us to miss out on the fact that God has always been with you. Perhaps your discernment button was pressed off. Praise God for covering us and keeping us in spite of ourselves.

Here is a simple little acronym for the word discern:

Determine to have His **Insight**. Be **Selective**.

Imitate His **Character**. Avoid the **Erroneous**. Don't get trapped by your own **Reasoning**. The Holy Spirit will always **Navigate** you into all Truth.

Hebrews 2:1 NIV

We must pay the most careful attention, therefore, to what we have heard, so that we do not drift away.

Genesis 28:16-17 NIV

When Jacob awoke from his sleep, he thought, "Surely the Lord is in this place, and I was not aware of it." He was afraid and said, "How awesome is this place! This is none other than the house of God; this is the gate of heaven."

Carelessness

Don't get stuck in a pattern of taking things or people for granted. I have seen this too much in the church.

Hebrews 2:3 NIV

How shall we escape if we ignore so great a salvation? This salvation, which was first announced by the Lord, was confirmed to us by those who heard him.

Revelation 3:11 NIV

I am coming soon. Hold on to what you have, so that no one will take your crown.

Ignorance

We can't be ignorant concerning the laws of life, destiny, and the Kingdom. We must be careful to honor and respect these three categories. I believe they will always keep us ahead of the curve of life.

Don't waste your life staying misinformed or uninformed. Ignorance always comes at a cost. So many Christians find themselves in the dark, fiddling and struggling through the process because of the absence of knowledge and direction on how to apply wisdom.

When it comes to your destiny, always note that the greatest investor will always be you. We can never expect people to invest in what we don't initially devote ourselves to.

And lastly, when it comes to things of the Kingdom of God, it's not enough to just be familiar with the principles of Jesus. We need to get familiar with the person of Jesus. This is so vital for us as citizens of the Kingdom of God. We must learn, know, and implement His statutes and laws that are relevant for advancing the Kingdom. At the end of the day, it's not our will but His will be done in us and on Earth.

Hosea 4:6 NIV

My people are destroyed from lack of knowledge.

Because you have rejected knowledge, I also reject you as my priests; because you have ignored the law of your God, I also will ignore your children.

2 Corinthians 2:11 NIV

… in order that Satan might not outwit us. For we are not unaware of his schemes.

Matthew 6:33 NIV

But seek first his kingdom and his righteousness, and all these things will be given to you as well.

Abuse/Misuse

People misuse and abuse power, money, and leadership too often in our culture today. Misappropriating and mishandling people and money is one sure way to lose your integrity and respect in the Body of Christ. Because everyone knows that in the church, we are often quick to judge, and not always as quick to pray.

Not everyone is intent on deceiving others. Some people have just had the wrong influences in their lives. Just use discretion and judgment when it comes to who you fellowship and connect with. We as a church must never forget that when we came to Jesus, we were by no means squeaky clean. We all needed to be forgiven and restored. Let's learn from the model of Jesus and restore, not destroy. No one is so far gone that grace and mercy cannot redeem them.

Just thought I'd add this right here, because we're in a world and church setting where there are imperfect people present. When people get off into this arena, their hearts begin to wax cold and their ears become desensitized to the things of the Spirit. I implore you to guard your gifts, and stay away from abuse and misuse.

Philippians 1:15 NIV
It is true that some preach Christ out of envy and rivalry, but others

out of good will.

2 Timothy 3:2-6 NIV

People will be lovers of themselves, lovers of money, boastful, proud, abusive, disobedient to their parents, ungrateful, unholy, without love, unforgiving, slanderous, without self-control, brutal, not lovers of the good, treacherous, rash, conceited, lovers of pleasure rather than lovers of God—having a form of godliness but denying its power. Have nothing to do with such people.

They are the kind who worm their way into homes and gain control over gullible women, who are loaded down with sins and are swayed by all kinds of evil desires, always learning but never able to come to a knowledge of the truth. Just as Jannes and Jambres opposed Moses, so also these teachers oppose the truth.

Hindered by Tests and Trials

Don't allow the tests and the trials you go through strip you down and stop you. Use them to glorify Him.

James 1:2-4 NIV

Consider it pure joy, my brothers and sisters, whenever you face trials of many kinds, because you know that the testing of your faith produces perseverance. Let perseverance finish its work so that you may be mature and complete, not lacking anything.

So many believers and people in general have so many reasons for not stepping out to accomplish things in life. I wanted to show here that even Abram had to relocate to find himself, as many of us might need to do at times.

I remember distinctively hearing the voice of the Lord one time when we had the ComEd (an electric utilities company) representative come out to update our meters. In that moment, I heard the Spirit of God say, "You must disconnect to reconnect." In other words, be willing to be put in a position of inconvenience to secure your next accomplishment in life. This text here sets up a platform shift and name change for Abram. I believe that many of you as readers right now are in a place where God is challenging you. Let me be that little voice in your ear that says, "You got this!"

Genesis 12:1-9 AMP
Now [in Haran] the Lord had said to Abram,
"Go away from your country,

And from your relatives

And from your father's house,

To the land which I will show you;

And I will make you a great nation,

And I will bless you [abundantly],

And make your name great (exalted, distinguished);

And you shall be a blessing [a source of great good to others];

And I will bless (do good for, benefit) those who bless you,

And I will curse [that is, subject to My wrath and judgment] the one who curses (despises, dishonors, has contempt for) you.

And in you all the families (nations) of the earth will be blessed."

So Abram departed [in faithful obedience] as the Lord had directed him; and Lot [his nephew] left with him. Abram was seventy-five years old when he left Haran.

Abram took Sarai his wife and Lot his nephew, and all their possessions which they had acquired, and the people (servants) which they had acquired in Haran, and they set out to go to the land of Canaan.

When they came to the land of Canaan, Abram passed through the land as far as the site of Shechem, to the [great] terebinth (oak) tree of Moreh.

Now the Canaanites were in the land at that time. Then the Lord appeared to Abram and said, "I will give this land to your descendants."

So Abram built an altar there to [honor] the Lord who had appeared to him. Then he moved on from there to the mountain on the east of Bethel, and pitched his tent, with Bethel on the west and Ai on the east; and there he built an altar to the Lord and called on the name of the Lord [in worship through prayer, praise, and thanksgiving].

Then Abram journeyed on, continuing toward the Negev (the South country of Judah).

"When we find a man meditating on the words of God, my friends, that man is full of boldness and is successful."
- Dwight L. Moody

Chapter 2

PERSPECTIVES OF COMFORT

"The comfort zone is a psychological state in which one feels familiar, safe, at ease, and secure. You never change your life until you step out of your comfort zone; change begins at the end of your comfort zone."

- Roy T. Bennett

According to Merriam Webster's Dictionary, the word comfort denotes:

To give strength and hope to: **CHEER**

To ease the grief or trouble of: **CONSOLE**

Synonyms: assure, cheer, console, reassure, solace, soothe.

Let's look for a minute at the word *comfort* from a Hebrew perspective.

In the Hebrew language the word ne•cha•ma is very unique. If you break its letters down, you'll receive two overlapping words:

no•ach (comfortable and resting) and cham or cha•ma (warm). Even the first word attests to the Hebrew origin of the English word 'comfort:' ne•cha•ma is then an offer of rest and easement to a troubled, suffering soul. Comfort, indeed, is best induced by warmth and restful conditions.

Now when it comes to this word comfort, I want you to see it from the angle of just settling in a set place or resting, not so much as the solace or peace you have after a life-altering experience. There are so many things that we often encounter as Christians or people of real faith. However, I am convinced that there is always more for us. We just have to be willing and able to see this. God has placed inside of us all a destiny which, of course, is made up of life situations and challenges that people often contend with. It is somewhere in the midst of all this that an assignment begins to unravel, and things that were uncertain begin to become certain—things that you didn't understand, all of a sudden, begin to make sense.

This word comfort, in reference to settling, is a struggle for many believers within the Body of Christ. I see this so often with people that have great potential but become dormant or just simply allow their dreams and desires to die because they are not willing to sacrifice and stretch. Many people fail and fall short in this department, but I believe that if you are reading this book right now, God is reminding you that you are more than capable of overcoming the opposition of settling. I've been guilty of this myself at times, as I'm quite sure many other leaders in the church world have.

I thank God for the men and women He has placed in my life that would not let my gift or assignment remain average. I have been very fortunate to know some amazing leaders in the Body of Christ; some of which, I've had the privilege of reaching out to or checking in with when I really need to. I believe this is so critical to success when it comes to the plan of God for your life.

It often makes me think of one of my favorite stories in the Bible, which of course is the story of Elijah and Elisha. There is so much we can draw from this example. Time and time again, this story serves as a template and reminder for me. You can never have double by remaining dormant! It will require you to be in the right position when it comes to promotion and elevation.

I know some people think it's automatic when someone lays hands on you, but that is so not true. It will always require your participation in the process of a promotion. This is why developing an ongoing relationship with God is vital, as well as connecting to a pastor, mentor, or coach who will help you develop the fortitude to get up from the quicksand that you've found yourself sinking in.

All of us can relate possibly to what I want to call "the quicksand effect." It happens through your intentions to do nothing in reference to your life. The quicksand effect happens when you stumble into something that no one else has pushed you into. You walked into it with your eyes wide open. The thing about quicksand, as I'm quite sure most of us know, is that it has been designed to trap you, pull you in using your own weight, and eventually consume your entire life. But I'm so grateful that even during the quicksand effect, if you allow it, there are people with the ability to pull you from that place of sinking to a level playing field. Thank God for destiny helpers!

★ ★ ★

THE LIFE OF MOSES

"Nothing great ever comes out of a comfort zone."

Let's begin to look at one of the most underrated prophets of the Old Testament, none other than that of Moses. He was the man of the hour in his time, but it wasn't without a cost! Moses was one of the first people to write portions of Scripture while John, the disciple of Jesus, was the last. Out of the forty plus authors who wrote certain parts of the Bible in a period of over 1500 years or so, Moses was among that alumni.

Perhaps no person in history, outside of Jesus Christ, has made such a profound impression on the world as Moses, the great lawgiver of Israel. He delivered an oppressed people from bondage, molded them into a renewed nation, and received revelation from God with new moral standards and laws.

Even so, God is the central focus through it all. Lessons in leadership are a hallmark of this study.

The Life of Moses can be divided into four parts:

- Deliverance from Egypt **(Exodus 1-18)**
- Israel at Sinai **(Exodus 19 to Leviticus 27)**
- The march toward Canaan **(Numbers)**
- Moses' final days **(Deuteronomy)**

Moses was the son of Amram and Yochebed of the tribe of Levi **(Exodus 2:1-10** and **6:20)**. Miriam and Aaron were his brother and sister. He was born in Egypt during a period in which the Israelites (the Hebrews) had become a threat to the Egyptians, simply because of their large population. The pharaoh at the time had ordered that every newborn male child of the Hebrews be cast into the Nile River to be drowned. So, Yochebed took her newborn son, placed him in a waterproof basket and hid him in the tall grass of the Nile. Meanwhile, Moses' sister, Miriam, hid herself and watched over the baby from a distance. A group of women and servants were bathing nearby. Pharaoh's daughter, hearing the baby crying, found and rescued him. She named him "Moses," meaning "drawn from the water." Her desire for a son was fulfilled; and she made certain that he had the best of everything, including an education.

Moses was brought up in the splendor of the Egyptian court as

Pharaoh's daughter's adopted son. Once he had grown to manhood, he became aware of his Hebraic roots and shared a deep compassion for his confined kinsmen. He became furious while witnessing an Egyptian master brutally beating a Hebrew slave, so he impulsively killed the Egyptian. Fearing Pharaoh's punishment, he fled into the desert of Midian and became a shepherd for Jethro, a Midianite priest (whose daughter Zipporah he later married). While tending the flocks on Horeb Mountain in the wilderness, he saw a bush burning yet not turning to ash. He heard a voice from within the bush telling him that he had been chosen to serve as the one who would lead the children of Israel out of Egypt. He was also told to declare the unity of God to his people. At that time, most Israelites were worshiping many gods. Moses was to tell them that there was only one God.

The tremendous responsibility of Moses' task, his shyness, and his own feeling of unworthiness brought forth a hesitancy and lack of confidence. The Divine answer was "Who made your tongue?" He was then assured that Aaron, his more talkative brother, would serve as his spokesman both to the children of Israel and to the Pharaoh. The promised destination for the Israelites' journey was a "land rich with milk and honey."

Moses returned to Egypt and persuaded the Hebrews to organize for a quick trip away from their Egyptian slave drivers. With Aaron, Moses informed Pharaoh that the God of the Hebrews demanded that Pharaoh free God's people. But Pharaoh refused to obey, bringing upon himself and his people ten terrible plagues (diseases that spread rapidly and can cause death) which Moses produced by using the miraculous staff he had received from God as a sign of his authority. The Egyptians suffered under the plagues of water turned into blood, frogs, gnats, flies, disease to their cattle, boils, hail, locusts, and darkness. Each plague was severe for the Egyptians, but the Israelites were left untouched.

The tenth plague is now celebrated as the Hebrew story of Passover. God sent the Angel of Death to kill the firstborn sons of the Egyptians—a proof of His immense strength and power. The Israelites protected their households by putting lamb's blood on their doorways so that the Angel of Death would know to pass over their homes. This last plague broke Pharaoh's resistance and moved him to grant the Hebrews permission to leave immediately. Moses thus found himself the leader of an undisciplined collection of slaves, Hebrew as well as non-Hebrew, escaping from the Egyptian territory toward freedom.

★ ★ ★

THE EXODUS MOMENT

Moses' immediate goal was Mt. Horeb, called Mt. Sinai, where God had first revealed Himself to Moses. The Hebrews came to the sacred mountain encouraged by the power they sensed in Moses. Summoned by God, Moses ascended the mountain and received the tablets of stone while the children of Israel heard the thundering forth of the Ten Commandments. Inspired, the people agreed to the conditions of the Covenant (agreement made between people and God).

Through forty years in the wilderness of Sinai, overcoming many obstacles, Moses led the horde of former slaves, shaping them into a nation. Many miracles happened along the way. When the Israelites stopped in front of the Red Sea with the Egyptian soldiers at their heels, it was Moses' raised staff that parted the Red Sea so they could cross. Once they had safely crossed, the sea crashed down, drowning many of their pursuers.

When food supplies ran out, God sent down what was called "manna" (spiritual food) every day for the nourishment of the

Israelites. Moses had to hear the Israelites complain about the food, the climate, and the slowness of their progress. Moses even had to hear the Israelites claim that Egypt had been better than this wilderness trip. When the people were in need of water, God told Moses to speak to a rock and water would spring from it. Moses' character was apparently worn down because, instead of following directions, the pressure caused him to strike the rock with his staff.

How many times in life have we dealt with pressure? Oftentimes, a lot of pressure can make you stagnate, complacent, or cause your purpose to be redirected. Perhaps you don't want to deal with something, someone, or a certain situation… so you just quit! Perhaps, when it comes to you moving out of a familiar place that you've been in all along, it comes down to making an important choice. You become reluctant or hesitate because of so many other factors that have now crippled your movement.

I hear people say too often that I can't do it, or I can't make a choice. At some point in all of our lives, there has to be a choice made. Whether good or bad, one has to be made. Let's all strive for the greater good.

"You can choose courage, or you can choose comfort. You cannot have both."

- Brene Brown

I have heard the expression "you win from within" probably hundreds of times. This has a lot of truth to it in so many ways. I have come to discover the greatest enemy is not those around you, it's often the one that is in you. A person can actually talk themselves into a season or talk themselves out of a season. You have the authority to determine if you will fail or succeed. The Bible declares in **Acts 1:8** that after the Holy Spirit is activated inside of you, you have the power. We see this innate ability in the sports arena as well as the entertainment arena. The power to not settle when you know there is more.

An individual with this type of personality makes a conscious determination that they have not come all this way to have nothing to show for it. So, they do whatever it takes to obtain the prize or reach their goal. It is that inward nature of being driven by the desire to succeed.

The truth of the matter is, there will always be obstacles and obstructions in our way. However, we must learn to plow and persevere through the process to achieve what some only just wish to have in life. We can never afford to become mediocre, accept being average, or only move when there is no risk. The greater the risk, the greater the reward, and everyone I know likes to be rewarded.

Our God, the Father, has called you to do something that will always cause you to stretch! You may be in this place now where you're stuck, but I charge you in Jesus' name to get up and grow; step out, and soar. If Peter could step out in the story of the harvest of fish, surely you can with the same or even greater results.

Moses was given a mandate by God to lead the children of Israel out of bondage in spite of his past, his insecurities, and his mental capacities. I believe many of us can relate to Moses to some extent. To a degree, he had such a great responsibility and weight upon his shoulders because of his assignment, not to mention the fact that he had to deal with Pharaoh.

"When it comes to your assignment, you will never elevate in it without the effort."

When you begin to discover that there is a comfort zone in your life, you begin to eliminate the excuses and accept the tasks before you. We can all relate this to some extent. I can recall so many instances where I've missed a moment or just barely made it because of procrastination, fear, timidity, or just simply not being bold enough. I believe that I personally would have done and accomplished more had I not been struggling in my faith and confidence departments.

I have seen so many believers who only go so far and wonder why they never really advance in life. I get it. Life is an enigma. It's often full of surprises. You just don't know how it will turn out, but you have to keep pressing.

Philippians 3:14 TPT
I run straight for the divine invitation of reaching the heavenly goal and gaining the victory-prize through the anointing of Jesus.

"If God has given all things their significance, and defined their bounds according to time, space, power, and number, and if He has appointed certain measurements to regulate things and times, biblical numbers must be symbolic, and be worthy of our study; and if a fit subject for study, the laws by which this symbolism of numbers is controlled, require to be ascertained."
- Patrick Fairbairn

I love the fact that we discover here in the life or tenure of Moses that there are four significant things depicted, as well as character traits he possessed as a leader. In biblical numerology, the number four is of great significance. As a matter of fact, in the Bible, there are certain numbers that are repeated often and are attached to vital religious events. Numerologists consider these numbers to be important; and thus, they are given special meanings that link the religion and the Scripture.

I would like to take just a moment to shed some light on the number "four." It represents the number of creativity or creation.

"Four" (cardinal number) was a sacred and complete number with the Hebrews, as well as with several other people groups. It occurs very frequently in the Old Testament and the New Testament.

It indicates completeness. We have "the four rivers of Paradise" **(Genesis 2:10)**; "the four winds of heaven" **(Ezekiel 37:9; Daniel 7:2, 8:8, 11:4; Zechariah 6:5)**; "the four winds" **(Matthew 24:31, Mark 13:27)**; "the four corners of the earth" **(Isaiah 11:12; Revelation 7:1, 20:8,** the King James Version "quarters"); "the four corners of the house" **(Job 1:19)**; Jephthah's daughter was bewailed "four days" a year **(Judges 11:40)**; "four cities" are mentioned several times in Joshua during the allotment of inheritances **(Joshua 19:7, 21:17-18, etc.)**; Nehemiah's enemies sent to him "four times" **(Nehemiah 6:4)**; "four kinds" (in the Revised Version margin, "families") of destroyers were threatened **(Jeremiah 15:3)**; Yahweh's "four sore judgments" **(Ezekiel 14:21)**; "four generations" were seen by Job **(Job 42:16)**; and "four things" are cited multiple times in **Proverbs 30**. Not to mention, there are four accounts of Jesus' life on Earth in the Gospels of Matthew, Mark, Luke, and John.

Here are some other interesting facts about the number "four". The word four has four letters. In the English language, there is no other number whose number of letters is equal to its value.

Many things are arranged in fours. There are four suits in a deck of cards, four points of the compass, and four phases of the moon. There are four wings on a bee, just to name a few.

However, according to certain individuals, the whole universe is built up by at least three forms, streams, or patterns of expression—namely: letters, numbers, and words. Somewhere in these three categories, there is a thread that connects us all to one word:

"purpose". There is nothing that has been created without a unique purpose for which it exists.

Ecclesiastes 3:11 AMP

He has made everything beautiful and appropriate in its time. He has also planted eternity [a sense of divine purpose] in the human heart [a mysterious longing which nothing under the sun can satisfy, except God]—yet man cannot find out (comprehend, grasp) what God has done (His overall plan) from the beginning to the end.

Chapter 3

QUALITIES OF A LEADER

"The self-discovery of your inherent leadership potential and an understanding of who you are and what you are meant to be are the keys to fulfilling your purpose from existence as a leader."

- Dr. Myles Monroe

Let's focus here just for a moment on some of the biblical qualities I have discovered that demonstrate what we should emulate as a prophet, as a leader, as a father, as a brother, and as a servant of God.

They demonstrate faith:

Romans 4:20-21 AMP

But he did not doubt or waver in unbelief concerning the promise of God, but he grew strong and empowered by faith, giving glory to God, being fully convinced that God had the power to do what He had promised.

From the moment God first appeared to him at the burning bush, Moses consistently turned his eyes toward God. As Moses responded to God in faith, the Lord developed his character over time as a mighty leader of His people.

They demonstrate a heart of prayer:

Luke 18:1 AMP

Now Jesus was telling the disciples a parable to make the point that, at all times, they ought to pray and not give up and lose heart.

Moses was a great man of prayer. Whether trapped between the Red Sea and the Egyptians or facing the people's rebellion in the desert, Moses laid his problems and his decisions before God.

They demonstrate humility:

Colossians 3:12 AMP

So, as God's own chosen people, who are holy [set apart, sanctified for His purpose] and well-beloved [by God Himself], put on a heart of compassion, kindness, humility, gentleness, and patience [which has the power to endure whatever injustice or unpleasantness comes, with good temper].

Moses showed that great leadership requires humility. When attacked, Moses did not defend himself but laid the matter before God and waited for God's vindication. "Now Moses was a very humble man, humbler than anyone else on the face of the earth." **(Numbers 12:3, AMP)**

They demonstrate courage:

Deuteronomy 31:6 AMP
Be strong and courageous, do not be afraid or tremble in dread before them, for it is the Lord your God who goes with you. He will not fail you or abandon you.

"Great leaders always seem to embody two seemingly disparate qualities. They are both highly visionary and highly practical."
- *John C. Maxwell*

When facing Pharaoh and subsequent challenges in the wilderness, Moses did not fear. Because Moses knew and trusted God completely, he had great courage in facing seemingly insurmountable challenges.

There was an uncanny uniqueness about him that caused him to stand out. In spite of his past and present, God had an ultimate plan for his future. He may not have been the most handsome or articulate, but he made himself of no reputation and made himself available.

The prophet Moses was picked out by God to be a leader for the children of Israel. I believe that was probably not on his radar at first.

How many of us in some form of ministry knew this is where we would end up? Most of us had our own agendas to an extent, but God's plan intervened. Being a leader is not something everyone is called to do. That's just the reality of it. Leaders are not made overnight, but they are pruned and processed, proven and prepared for the task that lies ahead.

The Bible is full of great examples of leaders from the Old Testament to the New Testament. Being a leader is not easy, and Moses discovered this first hand by needing to deal with people. Leaders stand alone, leaders pull out the best in others, leaders lead by example, leaders understand order and principles, and leaders learn to develop confidence in the midst of criticism.

His name literally denotes "one that was drawn out of". Many of you reading this right now know that God skipped over someone else in the family just to get to you. Real leaders don't have to advertise "I'm an apostle", "I'm a prophet", "I'm a pastor", "I'm a teacher", or "I'm an evangelist". Their lives display on a daily basis who they are without the need for a title to be verbalized.

"Truth is the most powerful force on earth because it cannot be changed." "You will always move toward anyone who increases you and away from anyone who makes you less." "Leaders make decisions that create the future they desire." "You will never possess what you are unwilling to pursue."
– Dr. Mike Murdock

"The shortest distance to leadership is service."
– Dr. Myles Monroe

★ ★ ★

CHARACTERISTICS OF A LEADER

Here are some great characteristics of a leader:

1. They are self-effacing servants.

Luke 22:26-27 AMP

But it is not to be this way with you; on the contrary, the one who is the greatest among you must become like the youngest [and least privileged], and the [one who is the] leader, like the servant. For who is the greater, the one who reclines at the table or the one who serves? Is it not the one who reclines at the table? But I am among you as the one who serves.

2. They do not disregard and overlook error.

Proverbs 16:12 KJV

"It is an abomination to kings to commit wickedness: for the throne is established by righteousness."

3. They are loyal, direct, and unbolted.

"Unbolted" – to open or unfasten by withdrawing a bolt. Some synonyms would be: unrestrained, free, unleashed, escaped, and unbound, just to name a few. Great leaders don't allow themselves to be bound by situations, issues, or environments. They find a solution or a way to accomplish the task at hand.

1 Thessalonians 5:14 NIV
And we urge you, brothers and sisters, warn those who are idle and disruptive, encourage the disheartened, help the weak, be patient with everyone.

4. They institute practices and principles that people will be obliged to follow.

Psalm 119:35 NIV
"Direct me in the path of your commands, for there I find delight."

Hebrews 13:7 NIV
Remember your leaders, who spoke the word of God to you. Consider the outcome of their way of life and imitate their faith.

Titus 1:7-8 NIV

Since an overseer manages God's household, he must be blameless—not overbearing, not quick-tempered, not given to drunkenness, not violent, not pursuing dishonest gain. Rather, he must be hospitable, one who loves what is good, who is self-controlled, upright, holy and disciplined.

5. They cover their people and lead them in the right direction.

Titus 2:1-10 NIV

You, however, must teach what is appropriate to sound doctrine. Teach the older men to be temperate, worthy of respect, self-controlled, and sound in faith, in love and in endurance.

Likewise, teach the older women to be reverent in the way they live, not to be slanderers or addicted to much wine, but to teach what is good. Then they can urge the younger women to love their husbands and children, to be self-controlled and pure, to be busy at home, to be kind, and to be subject to their husbands, so that no one will malign the word of God.
Similarly, encourage the young men to be self-controlled. In everything set them an example by doing what is good. In your teaching

show integrity, seriousness, and soundness of speech that cannot be condemned, so that those who oppose you may be ashamed because they have nothing bad to say about us.

Teach slaves to be subject to their masters in everything, to try to please them, not to talk back to them, and not to steal from them, but to show that they can be fully trusted, so that in every way they will make the teaching about God our Savior attractive.

6. They are concerned and compassionate.

Isaiah 16:5 NIV

"In love a throne will be established; in faithfulness a man will sit on it— one from the house of David — one who in judging seeks justice and speeds the cause of righteousness."

7. They don't provoke or push people to break character.

Matthew 15:13-14 TPT

Jesus replied, "Every plant that my heavenly Father didn't plant is destined to be uprooted. Stay away from them, for they're nothing more than blind guides. Do you know what happens when a blind man pretends to guide another blind man? They both stumble into a ditch!"

8. They are cognizant of current positions and considerate.

Acts 20:28 NIV

Keep watch over yourselves and all the flock of which the Holy Spirit has made you overseers. Be shepherds of the church of God, which he bought with his own blood.

9. They lead with peace of mind and holiness.

1 Timothy 2:1-2 NIV

"I urge, then, first of all, that petitions, prayers, intercession and thanksgiving be made for all people—for kings and all those in authority, that we may live peaceful and quiet lives in all godliness and holiness."

10. They know how to be reverent and courteous as a situation may permit itself.

2 Timothy 2:16 TPT

And avoid empty chatter and worthless words, for they simply add to the irreverence of those who converse in that manner.

Titus 1:9 NIV

He must hold firmly to the trustworthy message as it has been taught, so that he can encourage others by sound doctrine and refute those who oppose it.

11. They are diligent constantly and not conditionally.

Romans 12:7-8 TPT

If your grace-gift is serving, then thrive in serving others well. If you have the grace-gift of teaching, then be actively teaching and training others. If you have the grace-gift of encouragement, then use it often to encourage others. If you have the grace-gift of giving to meet the needs of others, then may you prosper in your generosity without any fanfare. If you have the gift of leadership, be passionate about your leadership. And if you have the gift of showing compassion, then flourish in your cheerful display of compassion.

12. They surround themselves with people that accomplished more than themselves.

Proverbs 11:14 NIV

For lack of guidance a nation falls, but victory is won through many advisers.

13. They are devoted to work based on love and not selfish motives.

Philippians 1:15-18 NLT

It's true that some are preaching out of jealousy and rivalry. But others preach about Christ with pure motives. They preach because they love me, for they know I have been appointed to defend the Good News. Those others do not have pure motives as they preach about Christ. They preach with selfish ambition, not sincerely, intending to make my chains more painful to me. But that doesn't matter. Whether their motives are false or genuine, the message about Christ is being preached either way, so I rejoice. And I will continue to rejoice.

14. They have the disposition to serve and are not driven by material things and money.

Titus 1:10-11 NLT

For there are many rebellious people who engage in useless talk and deceive others. This is especially true of those who insist on circumcision for salvation. They must be silenced, because they are turning whole families away from the truth by their false teaching. And they do it only for money.

15. They practice and model what they preach.

1 Peter 5:2-3 AMP

…shepherd and guide and protect the flock of God among you, exercising oversight not under compulsion, but voluntarily, according to the will of God; and not [motivated] for shameful gain, but with wholehearted enthusiasm; not lording it over those assigned to your care [do not be arrogant or overbearing], but be examples [of Christian living] to the flock [set a pattern of integrity for your congregation].

16. They have set skills and possess a level of integrity.

Psalm 78:72 NIV

"And David shepherded them with the integrity of heart; with skillful hands, he led them."

17. They are wise and not anxious.

Luke 14:31-32 NIV

Or suppose a king is about to go to war against another king. Won't he first sit down and consider whether he is able with ten thousand men to oppose the one coming against him with twenty thousand? If he is not able, he will send a delegation while the other is still a long way off and will ask for terms of peace.

18. Lastly, they are a great template for others to emulate.

1 Timothy 3:1-3 NIV

Here is a trustworthy saying: Whoever aspires to be an overseer desires a noble task. Now the overseer is to be above reproach, faithful to his wife, temperate, self-controlled, respectable, hospitable, able to teach, not given to drunkenness, not violent but gentle, not quarrelsome, not a lover of money.

Chapter 4

THE POWER OF SACRIFICING

We live in a society where it's okay to be average, okay to be different, okay to struggle, okay to live however and wherever we want, and one where it's okay to dishonor God. But, with all of this "freedom", there is no concept of sacrifice. It's almost like we have evolved into a society of entitlement with very little participation, a society that has high expectations but little effort, a society that wants you to solve all their issues and just hold out their hands for more. When I think of sacrificing, it brings to my mind the story of Abraham and Isaac. The love a father had for his son, but was still willing to give him up to please and honor God. We see a similar example with God the Father and His son Jesus.

Most of us are quite familiar with the story of Abram or Abraham. He had to make a sacrifice to get something he never had before, as do we all. Let me just say that when it comes to the things of God, we can never afford to settle or take for granted His grace and goodness towards us. All of us will have tests presented to us that will help determine what we are really capable of.

★ ★ ★

ABRAHAM'S TEST

Genesis 22:1-15 NIV

Some time later, God tested Abraham. He said to him, "Abraham!"

"Here I am," he replied.

Then God said, "Take your son, your only son, whom you love—Isaac—and go to the region of Moriah. Sacrifice him there as a burnt offering on a mountain I will show you."

Early the next morning Abraham got up and loaded his donkey. He took with him two of his servants and his son Isaac. When he had cut enough wood for the burnt offering, he set out for the place God had told him about. On the third day Abraham looked up and saw the place in the distance. He said to his servants, "Stay here with the donkey while I and the boy go over there. We will worship and then we will come back to you."

Abraham took the wood for the burnt offering and placed it on his son Isaac, and he himself carried the fire and the knife. As the two of them went on together, Isaac spoke up and said to his father Abraham, "Father?"

"Yes, my son?" Abraham replied.

"The fire and wood are here," Isaac said, "but where is the lamb for the burnt offering?"

Abraham answered, "God himself will provide the lamb for the burnt offering, my son." And the two of them went on together. When they reached the place God had told him about, Abraham built an altar there and arranged the wood on it. He bound his son Isaac and laid him on the altar, on top of the wood. Then he reached out his hand and took the knife to slay his son. But the angel of the Lord called out to him from heaven, "Abraham! Abraham!"

"Here I am," he replied.

"Do not lay a hand on the boy," he said. "Do not do anything to him. Now I know that you fear God, because you have not withheld from me your son, your only son."

Abraham looked up and there in a thicket he saw a ram caught by its horns. He went over and took the ram and sacrificed it as a burnt offering instead of his son. So Abraham called that place The Lord Will Provide. And to this day it is said, "On the mountain of the Lord it will be provided."

The angel of the Lord called to Abraham from heaven a second time and said, "I swear by myself, declares the Lord, that because you have done this and have not withheld your son, your only son, I will surely bless you and make your descendants as numerous as the stars in the sky and as the sand on the seashore. Your descendants will take possession of the cities of their enemies, and through your offspring all nations on earth will be blessed, because you have obeyed me."

If you will notice here in the story of Abraham, he had encountered a crossover moment for his life. I can only imagine the war in Abraham's heart that he had to contend with. However, everything that he encountered prepared him for the Crossover!

I believe at some time in all of our lives, a moment will come where we will have to sacrifice for the greater good or, in other words, put up or shut up! A time will come when you are put in a position that will require you to prove your passion or commitment to God and your assignment.

Things don't just happen automatically. Most of the things that occur in life were preceded by a choice. We have all learned that life isn't wish driven or desire driven—it's choice driven. We make choices every single day in life, whether we realize it or not.

Genesis 12:1-3 NIV

The LORD had said to Abram, "Go from your country, your people and your father's household to the land I will show you.

"I will make you into a great nation, and I will bless you; I will make your name great, and you will be a blessing.

I will bless those who bless you, and whoever curses you I will curse; and all peoples on earth will be blessed through you."

★★★

BATTLE OF WILLS

Basically, what I am stating here is that you should just surrender your will to His will. Let go of the wheel of fear, and take a hold of the wheel of faith. This will always assure and guarantee better results.

I remember growing up as a teenager in God like it was yesterday. I recall the times when I had to step out in faith. One specific time when I was still young in the Lord, a lady was dealing with unbearable pain. I remember while we were sitting in the car, the power of God came on me so heavily that I didn't know how to respond to it. I just know that my hands were vibrating what felt like ten times more than if they had fallen asleep. The anointing had fallen in that car we were in, and I said, "I don't know what to do." The young lady, who by the way was much older than me, said "Lay hands on me," and the pain left her body instantly!

There was also one other time I remember holding a baby in my hands who had a very high fever, over 100 degrees I believe. I asked the mother if it would be okay for me to pray, and she said yes! I began to pray, and was I nervous? You better believe I was! The Enemy was whispering in my ear, "Nothing is going to happen if you pray." All I can recall is praying in tongues for a moment as I spoke to the fever, "Be gone, in Jesus' name!" I literally felt that child's body come to a normal temperature. The power of God showed up and showed out once again.

There are so many other stories, but I just wanted to share these two to build your faith and help you step out of your comfort zone.

When I was much younger in the Lord, there was such a level of reverence and honor for the house of God. In those days, people knew how to press in and not stop until they heard from God. Some of them didn't let what people called them stopped them from loving and serving God.

Nowadays, it's almost like we have taken boldness and discarded it and have become intimidated by everyone and everything. If you allow people's opinions to matter, then you've already accepted your lot.

The opinions of others will only carry power to the degree of your acceptance. An opinion is just what it is… an opinion. It's not absolute. The only thing that is absolute is Jehovah God. He is the Alpha and the Omega, the beginning and the end, the Maker and Creator of the universe. When you begin to discover this, your life will become liberated. You were indeed created to excel, not to just accept the status quo.

If you ask me, it's often a form of witchcraft that makes you feel some kind of a way that you don't respond as a child of God is supposed to. Beware of this form of control in the church! I encourage you to not be controlled by control!

I recall stories of believers and many other great pioneers of the faith who have gone on to glory that have stepped out of their comfort zone time after time with signs and wonders of the supernatural. I have read of others, like the late Dr. Oral Roberts, Jack Coe Sr., Kenneth Hagin Sr., Kathryn Kuhlman, John G. Lake, Maria Woodworth-Etter, Agnes White Diffee, and Aimee Semple McPherson, just to name a few. There are so many other healing evangelists that have made a mark or deposit on the earth realm that cannot be erased.

All of these phenomenal men and women of God had something in common that I really need you to see. That is, they were all willing to go against the grain, step out of the box, and not allow the power of people's opinion stop them or limit them in pursuing their passion. Without fail, every time I read of these great patriarchs and matriarchs of faith, my faith is strengthened and challenged.

I remember being in prayer meetings on a Saturday morning as a young teenager and sensing the power of God. It has always been the norm for me, even as a teenager, to be in God's house or in some kind of prayer meeting environment. I have learned that spending time at His feet in prayer is the best route to go. There are no substitutes or alternatives. I believe that having developed a level of prayer in my life has given birth to a certain degree of boldness that I probably wouldn't have been exposed to if prayer wasn't a part of it. Prayer was not something I was made to do; I choose to do it. I knew if I wanted to hear and experience God, it was going to require me to leave my comfort zone.

"By leaving your comfort zone behind and taking a leap of faith into something new, you find out who you are truly capable of becoming."
- **Anonymous**

Proverbs 28:1 NLT

The wicked run away when no one is chasing them, but the godly are as bold as lions.

Acts 4:29 NLT

And now, O Lord, hear their threats, and give us, your servants, great boldness in preaching your word.

Ephesians 3:12 AMP

…in whom we have boldness and confident access through faith in Him [that is, our faith gives us sufficient courage to freely and openly approach God through Christ].

Luke 18:1 NIV

Then Jesus told his disciples a parable to show them that they should always pray and not give up.

1 Thessalonians 3:10 NIV

Night and day we pray most earnestly that we may see you again and supply what is lacking in your faith.

Back in the day, the denomination I was a part of was mostly always religious and scripted. There really wasn't a demonstration of the gifts of the Spirit as it is in some of our churches now. There has to be an awakening to the reality of God for this hour!

One of the only ways you can achieve anything in God is to simply dare to be different, dare not to be average, dare not to do the norm. People of God, the day for us to place the blame on others is over. In actuality, the disability or disconnect is with us.

As I stated earlier, you can't be or do anything great in God until you exit your comfort zone. Now, for some of us, we love to play it safe. But safe will never allow you to soar into the supernatural zone. This is the place where you're walking and demonstrating the Kingdom of God on Earth.

For so long, I too have struggled; but it wasn't until my associations began to shift, that my life began to swing in an upward motion. I'm speaking from experience here. I know what it feels like to get comfortable in a setting or to just be content with being the thermometer when God has called you to be the thermostat!

Always remember that as a Spirit-filled believer, you have the power and the authority to declare, to decree, and to prophesy the word of the Lord over your life. Ultimately, when it comes down to it at the end of the day, you are the main contributor to getting yourself out of a spiritual stupor, a comfort zone, or even a place that you've been too familiar with for too long. I challenge you to step so far out of your comfort zone that you forget how to get back!

As a believer, begin to see it and decree it. The seed of boldness may lay dormant in you now, but I declare it's getting ready to spring up out of you, in Jesus' name! Remember this: If it doesn't challenge you, it doesn't change you. Who's next to go and grow?

Job 22:28 AMP

You will also decide and decree a thing, and it will be established for you; and the light [of God's favor] will shine upon your ways.

Acts 1:8 AMP

But you will receive power and ability when the Holy Spirit comes upon you; and you will be My witnesses [to tell people about Me] both in Jerusalem and in all Judea, and Samaria, and even to the ends of the earth.

"When you're standing in the righteous place, authority will always accompany you."

PHARAOH WILL NOT FOLLOW YOU INTO YOUR FUTURE!

Oftentimes, many of us will face opposition and challenges in life. For whatever reason, there are times when some of the things we go through can't be identified. Sometimes, we can't even locate exactly what the issue is.

I just want to bring attention to something right here, especially in this season of your life. The Bible tells us that during the days of the prophet Moses, there was a ruler, a hard task master, a very insensitive individual, who only cared about his own agenda. This man was known as Pharaoh. He was known for inflicting pain on the children of Israel.

The story is a very interesting one because, I believe, somewhere within the story, some of us (if not all) can relate in some way. Life has not been fair to you; so-called friends walk away and forsake you; people use you and treat you unfairly. But what I have come to discover is that life has attached to it a word called "process".

It is so important to remember the passage from **John 10:10**.

John 10:10 NIV

The thief comes only to steal and kill and destroy; I have come that they may have life, and have it to the full.

Jesus did not come for you to be broke, robbing Peter to pay Paul, having more months than money, simply surviving, or at the very least, just barely getting by. He wants you to live a prosperous life and journey well, bless others along the way, extend grace and favor to someone in need, and encourage someone else with the Word of the Lord.

Grace is always available to those who need it and have a revelation of it. Imagine what our world would be like today without the grace of God. His grace is priceless and indescribable.

"What gives me the most hope every day is God's grace; knowing that His grace is going to give me the strength for whatever I face, knowing that nothing is a surprise to God."
- Rick Warren

I want to help shed a little light here so that you can understand this. Where you are right now is not where you are going.

Jeremiah 29:11 NIV

"For I know the plans I have for you," declares the Lord, "plans to prosper you and not to harm you, plans to give you hope and a future."

In other words… "your final outcome is income!"

The children of Israel had been dealing with Pharaoh for many years, as some you have been dealing with your own Pharaoh. But I want to challenge you to start today by declaring, "I will not stay stagnant or stuck another day in my life!"

Some people often become complacent where they are and just set up shop right there, if you will. Let me just encourage you here, child of God. You got this. As believers, we exist to live by faith, to step out even when we don't have all the details. We must continue to learn how to walk by faith and not by sight.

When it comes down to it, faith is the lifeline of the believer, as blood is the lifeline for mankind. We need air to breathe, water to drink, and food to eat. These are just some of the essentials which can relate to faith, hope, and wisdom. We need things to balance us naturally and spiritually.

I want to provoke a holy indignation in you that will stir you to strive, convict you to hold your course, and push you towards your purpose.

In the words of the late Dr. Myles Monroe, "You being born is evident that your purpose is necessary."

Remaining comfortable or just settling to coast through life will disqualify you from your original intent. Think about this. Out of over seven billion people on this planet, the number one question or statement on the mind of many is, where do I belong? What is my purpose?

One of the unfortunate things about this is that people get so used to an environment of not living fulfilled or satisfied that they just simply adapt and conform. They adapt to what people say and do; they conform to others' opinions of them.

Never feel as though you have to settle, to remain low key, dumbed down, or held back just to satisfy someone else's insecurity. Just because they can't handle or process what you're becoming, that's not on you, it's on them!

I believe we're in an hour right now where God is sending people across your path—which may be one of the reasons you're reading this. The God of Abraham, Isaac, and Jacob is present and has orchestrated your steps right to this book. This is why it's so important to have the spirit of prophecy released over your life. Being a recipient of prophetic ministry can save a derailing destiny from destruction.

Paul even validates this in Scripture. He informs the Corinthian church how important it is to know the purpose of prophecy. Many people will often miss out on God's plans because of the lack of having a prophetic voice present in their lives.

"The prophetic has the anointing and the ability to connect your mouth, mind, and purpose with the mind of God."

1 Corinthians 14:1-3 NIV

Follow the way of love and eagerly desire gifts of the Spirit, especially prophecy. For anyone who speaks in a tongue does not speak to people but to God. Indeed, no one understands them; they utter mysteries by the Spirit. But the one who prophesies speaks to people for their strengthening, encouraging and comfort.

2 Peter 1:19-21 NIV

We also have the prophetic message as something completely reliable, and you will do well to pay attention to it, as to a light shining in a dark place, until the day dawns and the morning star rises in your hearts. Above all, you must understand that no prophecy of Scripture came about by the prophet's own interpretation of things. For prophecy never had its origin in the human will, but prophets, though human, spoke from God as they were carried along by the Holy Spirit.

Chapter 6

PROPHETIC WORD

I just heard the Holy Spirit say, for I the Lord will plunder your adversaries in this season, for many of you have been under the mistaken impression that you're being set back. But know this, says the Lord, I am that I am, for what you are about to walk into in the coming year is something that has never happened in your bloodline. Did I not declare in **Habakkuk 1:5**, "I will work a work in your day that you will not believe, even though it's told to you!" I declare, your Pharaohs will be addressed, your Sauls will be slain, and you will recover that which you have lost says the Lord. For even as Moses encountered the burning bush says the Lord, I will cause you to experience a fresh fire; a fire unstoppable and undeniable.

And I even hear the Spirit of God say, every proverb or negative word spoken against you will lose its authority in this season, and you will experience a degree of strength that you haven't known in years, says the Lord.

Get ready, my sons and daughters. For every javelin that was been thrown at you will even fall to the ground. For My hand will rise strong at the close of this year.

Many of you will see massive momentum and massive increase! For even as Pharaoh ran behind Moses, and I caused a strong east wind to blow upon the waters, and they stood up on both sides, I will even cause for thee to cross over into a place called Canaan, a land that flows with milk and honey. For I am even allowing the Enemy to think he has you cornered, and just as I did it for Moses, I will also do it for thee. Your Pharaoh will drown this time, and you will not see this thing again! So rejoice, and know that if I am for you, I am more than the world that is against you, says the Lord.

For the time has come to cross over into increase, cross over into favor, cross over into wealth, and cross over into entrepreneurship! You will rise up in this hour because My glory will rest upon thee, and I declare massive moves in the Kingdom will be your portion, says the Lord!

Your past is just what it is… the past! Your Red Sea moment has ended, and your Exodus has begun! The Enemy has lost his grip and greatness is in front of you! I declare over you and your house that in this next season, you will not go empty, and everything that belongs to you will manifest right before your eyes.

So, I challenge you to go, and cross over into your new place. I know for most of you, it will be a sacrifice. But for the settlement that's on the other side, it will be well worth your stepping out of your comfort zone.

"You have been primed for purpose and through your persistence, you will encounter the promise."

LIBRARY OF BOLDNESS THAT BREAKS THE COMFORT ZONE

It will take a degree of boldness to submit our bodies to the Lord, especially in the culture we live in now.

Psalms 138:3 KJV

In the day when I cried thou answeredst me, and strengthenedst me with strength in my soul.

Proverbs 28:1 KJV

The wicked flee when no man pursueth: but the righteous are bold as a lion.

Acts 4:13 KJV

Now when they saw the boldness of Peter and John, and perceived that they were unlearned and ignorant men, they marvelled; and they took knowledge of them, that they had been with Jesus.

Acts 4:29 KJV

And now, Lord, behold their threatenings: and grant unto thy servants, that with all boldness they may speak thy word…

Acts 4:31 KJV

And when they had prayed, the place was shaken where they were assembled together; and they were all filled with the Holy Ghost, and they spake the word of God with boldness.

Acts 28:31 KJV

…preaching the Kingdom of God, and teaching those things which concern the Lord Jesus Christ, with all confidence, no man forbidding him.

Romans 12:1-2 KJV

I beseech you therefore, brethren, by the mercies of God, that ye present your bodies a living sacrifice, holy, acceptable unto God, which is your reasonable service.

2 Corinthians 3:12 NIV

Therefore, since we have such a hope, we are very bold.

Ephesians 3:12 KJV

In whom we have boldness and access with confidence by the faith of him…

Ephesians 6:19 KJV

And for me, that utterance may be given unto me, that I may open my mouth boldly, to make known the mystery of the gospel…

Philippians 1:20 KJV

According to my earnest expectation and my hope, that in nothing I shall be ashamed, but that with all boldness, as always, so now also Christ shall be magnified in my body, whether it be by life, or by death.

2 Timothy 1:6-7 KJV

Wherefore I put thee in remembrance that thou stir up the gift of God, which is in thee by the putting on of my hands.

Hebrews 4:16 KJV

Let us therefore come boldly unto the throne of grace, that we may obtain mercy, and find grace to help in time of need.

Hebrews 10:19-25 KJV

Having therefore, brethren, boldness to enter into the holiest by the blood of Jesus…

Hebrews 13:6 KJV

So that we may boldly say, The Lord is my helper, and I will not fear what man shall do unto me.

1 John 5:14 KJV

And this is the confidence that we have in him, that, if we ask any thing according to his will, he heareth us…

"THE CONFUSION"

"Confusion and impotence are the inevitable results when the wisdom and resources of the world are substituted for the presence and power of the Spirit."

- Samuel Chadwick

Chapter 8

TACTICS OF THE ENEMY

We must never let the Enemy deceive us into thinking that something is God's fault when in actuality, it's ours. We have played a part in this because we didn't do our due diligence in the matter! God is not and will never be the source of confusion. However, there is an adversary who will make every attempt and try everything possible to keep you perplexed in life. This is what we've learned in Sunday school, seminary, and the church institution. There is a real Devil that wants to keep you trapped in an enigma state.

Satan is the author of confusion: he seeks to cause chaos, disorder, death, and destruction.

1. 1 Corinthians 14:33 KJV

"For God is not the author of confusion, but of peace, as in all churches of the saints."

2. 1 Peter 5:8 NIV

"Be alert and of sober mind. Your enemy the Devil prowls around like a roaring lion looking for someone to devour."

3. 2 Corinthians 2:11 NIV

"…in order that Satan might not outwit us. For we are not unaware of his schemes."

4. Revelation 12:9-10 AMP

"And the great dragon was thrown down, the age-old serpent who is called the Devil and Satan, he who continually deceives and seduces the entire inhabited world; he was thrown down to the earth, and his angels were thrown down with him. Then I heard a loud voice in heaven, saying, 'Now the salvation, and the power, and the kingdom (dominion, reign) of our God, and the authority of His Christ have come; for the accuser of our [believing] brothers and sisters has been thrown down [at last], he who accuses them and keeps bringing charges [of sinful behavior] against them before our God day and night.'"

5. Ephesians 2:2 AMP

"…in which you once walked. You were following the ways of this world [influenced by this present age], in accordance with the *prince of the power of the air (Satan), the spirit who is now at work in the disobedient [the unbelieving, who fight against the purposes of God]."*

According to Merriam Webster's Dictionary, the word "confusion" denotes: the quality or state of being confused.
Synonyms: Bafflement, bamboozlement, befuddlement, bemusement, bewilderedness, bewilderment, confusedness, discombobulation, distraction, fog, scratching, maze, muddle, mystification, perplexity, puzzlement, tangle, whirl.

Joel 3:14 NIV

Multitudes, multitudes in the valley of decision! For the day of the Lord is near in the valley of decision.

Many of us as believers have often encountered attacks and setbacks from the adversary. Things that have occurred that make us second guess, become confused, or perhaps even wonder if we're ever going to prosper, ever going to succeed, ever going to be debt free, ever going to live a life where we are satisfied in God.

We must always know and understand that the Enemy would not be doing his job properly if everything was okay all the time for us. If you are reading this book right now, I believe there is something the Lord has to say to you about your situation. You are not alone! So many believers are impacted by a mental state of confusion, being indecisive, or just simply not knowing what the next step is supposed to be.

✶✶✶

RECLAIM AND RENEW

Let me encourage you in this moment. Being in a confused state is not a seal of destruction. It is not the end. It is merely a stop along the way to one's purpose and destiny. The mind plays a vital part in you either staying or soaring. It is so important that we exercise our mind with the Word of God. When a person becomes confused, often it is because they are disconnected from their original intent. God created us all to possess His promises. You may be in a place where you are now idle, but it's not you! Never allow your mind to have an extended stay in the courtyard of confusion. You are still an overcomer in Him. What you are contending with is just a temporary scenario. It is a situation… it's not who you really are!

Unfortunately, as Christians, we can get stuck and focus on that which is external. When this occurs, we become complacent. Whenever you are in a specific situation, it is always important to get a revelation.

I have seen this happen too often with Christians. We don't see through the lens of faith and into the spirit realm. You can be in a particular situation; but because you have no revelation, it doesn't affect who you are!

"Much confusion in the Christian life comes from ignoring the simple truth that God is far more interested in building your character than he is anything else."
- Rick Warren

I have discovered that throughout the church world, there has been a major attack on relationships, marriages, business partnerships, and even supposedly "covenant relationships" between brothers and sisters that are part of some tribe or group. Alliances are broken, and what was once sacred and honorable just isn't honorable anymore.

When did it ever become acceptable to be condescending or critical of others just because they have perhaps "outgrown" you? This by no means incites the character of Christ, but it does expose the depth and level of insecurities that are present in our culture, particularly in the church. That applies to any and all ethnicities as well.

I believe that this is a monumental prophetic season, and God has you on His mind now more than ever. Never allow the Enemy to convince you otherwise. I believe that this is the hour that God is going to break the spirit of confusion in the world and the Body of Christ. So much has gone on in the church and the world today that instead of developing unity, it has caused a degree of separation.

People are fighting when we should be uniting. All this does is create more confusion in the church. But I declare that God is going to raise up a generation that will possess another spirit like Joshua and Caleb.

Many of us in the church (or the secular world) can identify and relate that when there is confusion, there's no direction. But if God can do the miraculous with Moses, He can do it with you too.

Perhaps you've dug yourself into a hole where you need help to get out of this. Perhaps like the saying goes, "I've fallen, and I can't get up." I really sense by the Spirit of the Lord that God's strong hand is about to manifest mightily in this New Year!

Exodus 23:27 NIV

"I will send my terror ahead of you and throw into confusion every nation you encounter. I will make all your enemies turn their backs and run."

I was so stirred to pen the words that were on my heart (and I believe the mind of God) for this season in the Body of Christ. I know that you have been in a place unlike you've probably ever been before. At some point in your life, it appeared as though everything was going well. Then, all of a sudden, you matured from a place of mistaken identity and discovered your assignment. This is when the indifference kicked in on a whole new level.

Well, I have some amazing news for you, child of God. The Father really does see and know all, and He is always faithful.

"God will lock the advancement of your adversaries and advance you."

Through the story of Moses and extending to Joshua, we understand that Canaan was the land that was promised to the children of Israel. As believers, we must know that the Adversary does not want you to encounter the promises of God. So, he will attempt, in any capacity, to get you to confess that it's never going to happen. My father was broke, my mom was broke, my family was broke, and so I guess I will be as well. But as I often say, "the Devil is a liar and his mother-in-law too". There are so many blessings and promises that we have yet to tap in to.

One of the reasons so many Christians don't walk in the promises of God is because of a wrong perspective that is interpreted from His Word. God is and will always be a God of divine order. You can't serve God from your soul; you have to serve Him through your spirit, or better yet, the Spirit of God.

John 16:12-15 NIV

"I have much more to say to you, more than you can now bear. But when he, the Spirit of truth, comes, he will guide you into all the truth. He will not speak on his own; he will speak only what he hears, and he will tell you what is yet to come. He will glorify me because it is from me that he will receive what he will make known to you. All that belongs to the Father is mine. That is why I said the Spirit will receive from me what he will make known to you."

When it comes to the spirit of confusion, it is deceptive, it is distracting, and it will disconnect you from balance and order. That is why we need people like a Moses, like a Joshua, like an Elijah, or like a David, to keep us on course. I'm quite sure those of you who have been leaders in any shape, form, or fashion know exactly what I am talking about.

The Body of Christ is full of people who don't even realize that some of their decisions open the door wide to the spirit of confusion. This spirit carries an undercurrent of a lack of foundation. When it comes to a "foundation", I have found that if there is much strength, you're not easily swayed or moved. You can't build a house, let alone your destiny in God, if you're never settled long enough for it to really process itself.

I think it's important to note here, you can't expect to build a legacy without enduring longevity. A foundation based upon the Word will certainly minimize, if not completely eliminate the confusion in your life.

The seasoned saints used to sing a song relative to this subject when I was a teenager. "On Christ, the Solid Rock I stand; all other ground is sinking sand." Believe it or not, you can be stuck in a repetitive cycle and not even be aware that you're just like that gerbil, running around inside the wheel and never gaining or accomplishing anything.

We need our spiritual fathers and mentors to speak into our lives, to assist us in going the right direction. Another thing I've learned is that speed is not nearly as important as direction is! You can be doing something in your life, it can even be something for God, but your direction might be off. I want to challenge you to get off the spinning wheel of life. Meet new people, not everybody, just the right somebody!

1 Corinthians 14:40 NIV

But everything should be done in a fitting and orderly way.

I get that we're in an apostolic and prophetic culture; but having too many prophetic and spiritual gifts with no character is like a ticking time bomb, ready to go off any second. And it will do great damage. We just can't get by on a few prophetic words here and there. The Word of God must be active in our lives on a daily basis. It's not when and where we think we need it, but in everything we do or say. Everywhere we go, we must have His Word accompanying us as believers.

Matthew 6:11-13 AMP

Give us this day our daily bread.

And forgive us our debts, as we have forgiven our debtors [letting go of both the wrong and the resentment].

And do not lead us into temptation, but deliver us from evil. [For yours is the kingdom and the power and the glory forever.]

Matthew 4:4 NIV

Jesus answered, "It is written: 'Man shall not live on bread alone, but on every word that comes from the mouth of God.'"

Psalms 119:105-112 MSG

By your words I can see where I'm going; they throw a beam of light on my dark path. I've committed myself and I'll never turn back from living by your righteous order. Everything's falling apart on me, GOD; put me together again with your Word. Festoon me with your finest sayings, GOD; teach me your holy rules. My life is as close as my own hands, but I don't forget what you have revealed. The wicked do their best to throw me off track, but I don't swerve an inch from your course. I inherited your book on living; it's mine forever—what a gift! And how happy it makes me! I concentrate on doing exactly what you say—I always have and always will.

Psalms 119:130 KJV

The entrance of thy words giveth light; it giveth understanding unto the simple.

"Lack of clarity will keep a rhythm of confusion present in your life."

Proverbs 3:5-6 NIV

Trust in the LORD with all your heart and lean not on your own understanding; in all your ways submit to him, and he will make your paths straight.

★ ★ ★

STILL SMALL VOICE

The Holy Spirit whispered something to me earlier today and said, "John, people that often say I have a peace about where I am may not realize that this kind of peace can often be disguised as determination and ambition."

There is a false sense of peace that breeds more error and misalignment. We must understand, people of God, He has an assignment of alignment for you; on the other hand, the Devil's plan is misalignment! If he's able to keep you in a cycle of confusion and chaos, that's exactly what he will do. Peace in God will never go against His order and His word.

I know as far as ministry goes, some of us often struggle with "should I stay or should I go?" Is this God or is this just good? Is it the right timing or not? I believe the Enemy feeds on disorder and confusion. He's always in a place and position of pointing back to the Lord and saying, "I told you so God, they don't really want to grow, they don't really want to live for you, they don't really want to be submitted or be accountable." The sad thing here is that the cycle will continue until this thing is put to rest in our lives.

While I'm talking to you, the Holy Spirit is talking to me as well. None of us are exempt from being trapped in certain places where we just don't know what to do. However, there is always hope in God. Even though right now, you may be feeling some kind of way—the walls closing in around you, things not happening the way you wanted them to—God has His angels at attention to go to war on your behalf.

One of my "go-to" Scriptures, or stories if you will, involves King David. He was a warrior, a worshiper, and believed in the Word of the Lord.

"Confusion, if not overthrown by courage and focus, will eventually cause you to crash."

Psalms 20:1-9 MSG
GOD answer you on the day you crash,
The Name, God-of-Jacob, put you out of harm's reach,
Send reinforcements from Holy Hill,
Dispatch from Zion fresh supplies,

Exclaim over your offerings,

Celebrate your sacrifices,

Give you what your heart desires,

Accomplish your plans.

When you win, we plan to raise the roof

And lead the parade with our banners.

May all your wishes come true!

That clinches it—help's coming,

An answer's on the way;

Everything's going to work out.

See those people polishing their chariots,

And those others grooming their horses?

But we're making garlands for GOD our God.

The chariots will rust,

Those horses pull up lame—

And we'll be on our feet, standing tall.

Make the king a winner, GOD;

The day we call, give us your answer.

Hebrews 12:2 TPT

We look away from the natural realm and we focus our attention and expectation onto Jesus who birthed faith within us and who leads us forward into faith's perfection. His example is this: Because his heart was focused on the joy of knowing that you would be his, he endured the agony of the cross and conquered its humiliation, and now sits exalted at the right hand of the throne of God!

A MEPHIBOSHETH MOMENT

It so happened that King Saul's son, Jonathan, had a son who was maimed in both feet. When he was five years old, the report on Saul and Jonathan came from Jezreel. His nurse picked up Mephibosheth and ran; but in her hurry to get away, she fell, and the boy was maimed **(2 Samuel 4:4)**.

This young man named Mephibosheth had a traumatic experience that caused him to spiral into a state of depression and isolation. He became confused and forgot who he was as a kid in the king's house. He eventually finds himself in a very low place called Lo Debar.

A Mephibosheth Moment implies that you may have been dropped in life, but you can't afford to stay in that low place, Lo Debar—feeling sad, defeated, depressed, and left alone. What follows is an amazing story of restoration and crossing over.

2 Samuel 9:3-7 MSG

The king (David) asked, "Is there anyone left from the family of Saul to whom I can show some godly kindness?"

Ziba told the king, "Yes, there is Jonathan's son, lame in both feet."

"Where is he?"

"He's living at the home of Makir son of Ammiel in Lo Debar."

King David didn't lose a minute. He sent and got him from the home of Makir son of Ammiel in Lo Debar.

When Mephibosheth son of Jonathan (who was the son of Saul), came before David, he bowed deeply, abasing himself, honoring David.

David spoke his name: "Mephibosheth."

"Yes sir?"

"Don't be frightened," said David. "I'd like to do something special for you in memory of your father Jonathan. To begin with, I'm

returning to you all the properties of your grandfather Saul. Furthermore, from now on you'll take all your meals at my table."

When you have gone through life and have experienced being dropped and abandoned with no one to help you with your identity or to fulfill your purpose, you can often find yourself walking through the doors of uncertainty and get lost in the hallways of despair.

I believe that several of you are in an unusual and unidentifiable place like Mephibosheth was. But know that God has you on His mind, and He's about to send someone your way to bring you up out of that Lo Debar place. Get ready to get up, and cross over.

"THE CONDUCT"

"Good conduct is revealed in the pursuit of balance and order."

Chapter 10

THE CODE

What is a Christian code or guide post for conduct, you may ask?

The definition of conduct is the manner in which a person behaves, especially on a particular occasion or in a particular context.

Synonyms: administer, administrate, carry on, control, direct, govern, guide, handle, keep, manage, operate, overlook, oversee, preside (over), regulate, run, steward, superintend, supervise, tend to.

"The great guardian principle of all conduct in the church of God is personal responsibility to the Lord."
- **John Nelson Darby**

One of the main ways we as believers can monitor and maintain our Christian conduct is by developing a depth and discipline for God's written Word and following this ready-made template.

The Ten Commandments: The Christian Code of Conduct examines the commandments of God and how they can apply to the everyday life of a Christian. The Ten Commandments are the Christian's code of conduct that separates us from the rest of the world and serve as a barometer of our allegiance to the Creator of the universe. It sets our response apart from those who are non-believers. As Christians, we are charged by God to a higher standard or requirement of living.

Theology is a serious quest for the true knowledge of God, undertaken in response to His self-revelation, illumined by Christian tradition, manifesting a rational inner coherence, issuing in ethical conduct, resonating with the contemporary world and concerned for the greater glory of God.
- ***John Stott***

Conduct is a word we don't see enough of at times, especially when it comes to the secular, but also in the church of the living God. However, we know it is a necessity that we cannot overlook or take for granted.

I strongly believe that whether you're in the marketplace or the church, you too can walk in a much greater degree of honor and respect when you value conduct. It makes you a better asset to a corporation or church institution. This even applies to our relationships, marriages, friendships, and partnerships. When you practice conduct on a consistent basis, your conduct takes on the form of glue, in the sense that it holds and keeps you in place.

No one wants to be with someone or face something that demonstrates the characteristics of instability or bad choices. So often when this happens, there is a spiral of your faith. Your faith is not as strong as it should be. I have learned over the years, the stronger your faith is reflects the revelation that you possess for God and His Word.

Conduct is not to be considered a crutch or restriction but to serve as a guide post. Quite a few people struggle with discipline and being diligent in the things that will ensure their success, if they just stay the course. This is why I am always there to encourage the students that I mentor. It is so important to have someone to journey through life with until you reach your destination. As much as we sometimes hate to admit it, we all need help! The Apostle Paul had Silas, King Saul had Samuel, David had Jonathan, and Ruth had Naomi.

Let me say this again for the record, destiny helpers are being released as you are reading this book. Say it with me: "My destiny helpers are on the way, in Jesus' name!"

So many people want to have the prestige and power, but there is no power without pressure. Power only works when it's accountable to authority, not the other way around.

Can you believe that people actually demand some degree of authority as well? Authority is not something you can just demand at the drop of a hat. There must be a willingness to display integrity.

Let me just say it like this. You can't walk where you haven't lived. There is so much that is on the other side of obedience.

1 Samuel 15:22 AMP

Samuel said, "Has the Lord as great a delight in burnt offerings and sacrifices as in obedience to the voice of the Lord? Behold, to obey is better than sacrifice, and to heed [is better] than the fat of rams."

★★★

POSITION AFFECTS CONDUCT

"Your faith is often small or insignificant because of a lack of awareness of His authority. Become more aware of His authority and your life will shift and never settle again!"

I believe that as Christians, when we understand our position and place in the Lord, our conduct will change, our life will change, and our walk with the Lord will strengthen. I believe that sometimes, the challenges lie in knowing who you are and who you're connected to. It really does make a world of difference when you discover this. You conduct yourself in a different way, your conversation is different, your thoughts are different, your mannerisms are different, even the way you all out present yourself to others will be different.

When it all comes down to it at the end of the day, you are what you digest! What you consume a majority of the time will often reflect in your conduct.

"Accountability to alignment is what will keep you in your assignment."

When there is a lack of accountability, you become exposed to error. The things that you should do, you find yourself not doing; you find yourself with the people you shouldn't be with, and even in places you shouldn't be in.

Here are several key points that I must share about accountability:

You must be accountable to Wisdom!

You must be accountable to Worshiping Him regularly and not yourself or others!

You must be accountable to Waiting on His timing and season!

You must be accountable to Working the specific assignment He's given you and not concern or measure yourself with others!

You must always be accountable to the Word of God!

Chapter 11

THE BATTLE BETWEEN THE SOUL AND THE SPIRIT

Romans 7:14-19 AMP

We know that the Law is spiritual, but I am a creature of the flesh [worldly, self-reliant—carnal and unspiritual], sold into slavery to sin [and serving under its control]. For I do not understand my own actions [I am baffled and bewildered by them]. I do not practice what I want to do, but I am doing the very thing I hate [and yielding to my human nature, my worldliness—my sinful capacity]. Now if I habitually do what I do not want to do, [that means] I agree with the Law, confessing that it is good (morally excellent). So now [if that is the case, then] it is no longer I who do it [the disobedient thing which I despise], but the sin [nature] which lives in me. For I know that nothing good lives in me, that is, in my flesh [my human nature, my worldliness—my sinful capacity]. For the willingness [to do good] is present in me, but the doing of good is not. For the good that I want to do, I do not do, but I practice the very evil that I do not want.

As long as you are in the flesh, there is always going to be something striving for your attention and time. As human beings, we are all wired differently. However, flesh is flesh, and soul is soul. Your soul has a mind of its own, as does your spirit man. Your soul has several familiar components, such as: your mind, your will, your emotions, your intellect, and your imagination. The spirit, on the other hand, is wired by the Holy Spirit.

Romans 8:14 AMP

For all who are allowing themselves to be led by the Spirit of God are sons of God.

When you allow yourself to get trapped in the soulish realm, you give and permit demonic access to principalities and powers that can destroy you.

Let's look at a few biblical examples here:

Moses had a few mental moments, as we all do at times. We can remember when his conduct shifted in **Exodus 2:11-15** with the murder wrap situation that caused him to flee out of town. But he also dealt with disobedience in the sense that he was supposed to speak to the rock first, not strike it in **Numbers 20:8-12**.

Numbers 20:8-12 AMP

"Take the rod; and you and your brother Aaron assemble the congregation and speak to the rock in front of them, so that it will pour out its water. In this way you shall bring water for them out of the rock and let the congregation and their livestock drink [fresh water]."

So Moses took the rod from before the LORD, just as He had commanded him; and Moses and Aaron gathered the assembly before the rock. Moses said to them, "Listen now, you rebels; must we bring you water out of this rock?" Then Moses raised his hand [in anger] and with his rod he struck the rock twice [instead of speaking to the rock as the LORD had commanded]. And the water poured out abundantly, and the congregation and their livestock drank [fresh water]. But the LORD said to Moses and Aaron, "Because you have not believed (trusted) Me, to treat Me as holy in the sight of the sons of Israel, you therefore shall not bring this assembly into the land which I have given them."

Another example would be the Apostle Paul. Prior to his conversion from Saul of Tarsus, he had a major conduct issue. If you refer to the story in the Book of Acts, you will see what I mean.

Acts 9:1-9 AMP

Now Saul, still breathing threats and murder against the disciples of the Lord [and relentless in his search for believers], went to the high priest, and he asked for letters [of authority] from him to the synagogues at Damascus, so that if he found any men or women there belonging to the Way [believers, followers of Jesus the Messiah], men and women alike, he could arrest them and bring them bound [with chains] to Jerusalem. As he traveled he approached Damascus, and suddenly a light from heaven flashed around him [displaying the glory and majesty of Christ]; and he fell to the ground and heard a voice [from heaven] saying to him, "Saul, Saul, why are you persecuting and oppressing Me?" And Saul said, "Who are You, Lord?" And He answered, "I am Jesus whom you are persecuting, get up and go into the city, and you will be told what you must do." The men who were traveling with him [were terrified and] stood speechless, hearing the voice but seeing no one. Saul got up from the ground, but though his eyes were open, he could see nothing; so they led him by the hand and brought him into Damascus. And he was unable to see for three days, and he neither ate nor drank.

★ ★ ★

DISCIPLINE AND DILIGENCE

Philippians 4:8-9 MSG

Summing it all up, friends, I'd say you'll do best by filling your minds and meditating on things true, noble, reputable, authentic, compelling, gracious—the best, not the worst; the beautiful, not the ugly; things to praise, not things to curse. Put into practice what you learned from me, what you heard and saw and realized. Do that, and God, who makes everything work together, will work you into his most excellent harmonies.

Hebrews 11:6 AMP

But without faith it is impossible to [walk with God and] please Him, for whoever comes [near] to God must [necessarily] believe that God exists and that He rewards those who [earnestly and diligently] seek Him.

There are two words implied here in this text that I need for you to see hidden in the word diligence. They are *discipline* and *discernment!*

The word "diligence" according to Merriam Webster's Dictionary denotes: steady, earnest, and energetic effort; persevering application.

"Diligence is a Doorway to walking in your Destiny; practice it Daily, and you will never become Dormant or Distracted."

Chapter 12

LIBRARY OF CONDUCT

Ephesians 5:15-17 AMP

Therefore see that you walk carefully [living life with honor, purpose, and courage; shunning those who tolerate and enable evil], not as the unwise, but as wise [sensible, intelligent, discerning people], making the very most of your time [on earth, recognizing and taking advantage of each opportunity and using it with wisdom and diligence], because the days are [filled with] evil. Therefore do not be foolish and thoughtless, but understand and firmly grasp what the will of the Lord is.

Philippians 1:27 AMP

Only [be sure to] lead your lives in a manner [that will be] worthy of the gospel of Christ, so that whether I do come and see you or remain absent, I will hear about you that you are standing firm in one spirit [and one purpose], with one mind striving side by side [as if in combat] for the faith of the gospel.

Philippians 2:5 AMP

Have this same attitude in yourselves which was in Christ Jesus [look to Him as your example in selfless humility]…

Colossians 4:5-6 AMP

Conduct yourself with wisdom in your interactions with outsiders (non-believers), make the most of each opportunity [treating it as something precious]. Let your speech at all times be gracious and pleasant, seasoned with salt, so that you will know how to answer each one [who questions you].

1 Timothy 3:14-15 AMP

I hope to come to you before long, but I am writing these instructions to you in case I am delayed, so that you will know how people ought to conduct themselves in the household of God, which is the church of the living God, the pillar and foundation of the truth.

1 Timothy 4:12 AMP

Let no one look down on [you because of] your youth, but be an example and set a pattern for the believers in speech, in conduct, in love, in faith, and in [moral] purity.

Hebrews 13:7 AMP

Remember your leaders [for it was they] who brought you the word of God; and consider the result of their conduct [the outcome of their godly lives], and imitate their faith [their conviction that God exists and is the Creator and Ruler of all things, the Provider of eternal salvation through Christ, and imitate their reliance on God with absolute trust and confidence in His power, wisdom, and goodness].

1 Peter 1:13-16 AMP

So prepare your minds for action, be completely sober [in spirit—steadfast, self-disciplined, spiritually and morally alert], fix your hope completely on the grace [of God] that is coming to you when Jesus Christ is revealed. [Live] as obedient children [of God]; do not be conformed to the evil desires which governed you in your ignorance [before you knew the requirements and transforming power of the good news regarding salvation]. But like the Holy One who called you, be holy yourselves in all your conduct [be set apart from the world by your godly character and moral courage]; because it is written, "You shall be holy (set apart), for I am holy."

1 Peter 2:12 AMP

Keep your behavior excellent among the [unsaved] Gentiles [con-

duct yourself honorably, with graciousness and integrity], so that for whatever reason they may slander you as evildoers, yet by observing your good deeds they may [instead come to] glorify God in the day of visitation [when He looks upon them with mercy].

1 Peter 3:1 and 7 AMP

In the same way, you wives, be submissive to your own husbands [subordinate, not as inferior, but out of respect for the responsibilities entrusted to husbands and their accountability to God, and so partnering with them] so that even if some do not obey the word [of God], they may be won over [to Christ] without discussion by the godly lives of their wives… In the same way, you husbands, live with your wives in an understanding way [with great gentleness and tact, and with an intelligent regard for the marriage relationship], as with someone physically weaker, since she is a woman. Show her honor and respect as a fellow heir of the grace of life, so that your prayers will not be hindered or ineffective.

"THE CLEAR VISION"

"The best way to succeed is to have a specific Intent, a clear Vision, a plan of Action, and the ability to maintain Clarity. Those are the Four Pillars of Success. It never fails!"

- Steve Maraboli

Chapter 13

HAVING CLARITY

According to Merriam Webster's Dictionary, the word "clarity" denotes: the quality or state of being clear.

Synonyms: clearness, limpidity, limpidness, translucence, translucency, transparency.

"Clarity is when you can use both eyes and ears naturally and spiritually to discern what's in front of you, around you and in you, and fulfill your assignment."

Proverbs 4:7-12 AMP

The beginning of wisdom is: Get [skillful and godly] wisdom [it is preeminent]!

And with all your acquiring, get understanding [actively seek spiritual discernment, mature comprehension, and logical interpretation].

Prize wisdom [and exalt her], and she will exalt you;

She will honor you if you embrace her.

She will place on your head a garland of grace;

She will present you with a crown of beauty and glory.

Hear, my son, and accept my sayings,

And the years of your life will be many.

I have instructed you in the way of [skillful and godly] wisdom;

I have led you in upright paths.

When you walk, your steps will not be impeded [for your path will be clear and open];

And when you run, you will not stumble.

I want to take an opportunity here to share some of my history as to where I used to be and where I am now. Believe me, it has been a process. It took me coming to the place where I realized God has a specific plan for my life. The more I went after Him and got closer to Him, the more my life began to make sense. I walked away from confusion and through the door of clarity.

"If you ever plan to walk in your assignment, it will require you to go through the process of elimination to secure your destiny."

I can remember as a young man, being on fire for God but still not really having direction for my life. There was a point in my life when I figured I would try majoring in psychology, or perhaps even become a fireman. Of course, so much was going on in my little world at that time. I was struggling with low self-esteem, rejection, abandonment, and isolation at times, just to name a few.

Who would have ever thought someone like me would rise from the ashes of society and stereotypes. I am truly one of the people The Winans sang about: "Millions didn't make it, but I was one of the ones who did."

At one time in my life, I was very shy and withdrawn. Even now to some degree, there's still a little bit of the shyness hiding inside.

Passivity has been a principality of my past that often tries to rear its ugly head to cripple or stop me.

However, we can never let something such as passivity or procrastination rob us of our purpose! I'm quite sure I'm not the only one who has dealt with these things. Back then, I didn't have a revelation of the Holy Spirit that lives in me as I do now.

From growing up in a gang-infested neighborhood, low income housing, single parents, and prostitution all around, the odds were already stacked against me to become a product of my environment. I remember it like it was yesterday. Gang wars, people fighting over territory or turf. It was unfortunately the norm for us. We actually had a major gang lord who had their place right around the corner from where I used to live as a kid.

Not knowing and continuing to not know what it is you are here to do is not good at all. Everyone on this planet is here for a reason, for a purpose. And although things may be bad all around you, this is when you discover that God loves you and will send someone into your life to pull you out of the plan of the Enemy. Praise God!

"Clarity starts with an initial choice that will eventually connect and point you towards your destiny."

At certain seasons of my life, I literally have found myself walking through a wilderness experience. There are many trees in a wilderness environment, which often limit your visibility; it's often several sounds and other noises you hear as well. Feeling lost, alone, in a daze or confused. In the wilderness, there's often an environment of darkness, things that cause you to question your sanity or a place of isolation. It's never and will never be a good place to be.

But just as God did it for the children of Israel, and even myself, He can and will do the same for you… if you allow Him to.

★★★

WALKING THROUGH THAT WILDERNESS

"There can often be many voices in the wilderness, but there's only one voice that can deliver you."

John 10:27-28 NIV

My sheep listen to my voice; I know them, and they follow me. I give them eternal life, and they shall never perish; no one will snatch them out of my hand.

There are times in life when you may have felt as I did. Perhaps you felt as though you have been dealt a short hand of cards, or maybe you wish you were in another world where things could have been different. The reality is that we have all faced a life full of decisions. And the truth of the matter is, as long as you are on this earth, you will continue to be presented with choices.

I can recall when I first gave my life to the Lord as a teenager. A lot of so-called friends didn't get it. They didn't (or couldn't) understand. But even in the midst of this, I knew inwardly that a new journey had begun, and it would require the right kind of people in my life to help me get to where I was supposed to be.

"Living life as a believer should always be fulfilling and enjoyable and not disappointing and frustrating."

Proverbs 20:5 MSG

Knowing what is right is like deep water in the heart; a wise person draws from the well within.

Chapter 14

ARISE FROM THE JUNIPER TREE

I want to speak to many of you who feel the hand of the Lord is mighty upon, but you are literally in a mental and physical battle. You cannot allow the Enemy to defeat and derail you from your destiny. Many of you may have been impacted and infected by the setbacks of life; but I declare that every setback is a setup for a greater comeback. You will arise from this grave of guilt, shame, and lack of confidence and boldness. You will come forth as Lazarus did when Jesus called his name. I challenge you right where you are, man of God, woman of God; it's time to get up from under the Juniper tree!

"Graves were designed to bury the dead and not your gift, continue to flourish in your gift and own it."

One of the most relevant stories in the Bible that involves someone dealing with a lack of clarity and identity is that of the prophet Elijah.

The prophet Elijah was moving in miracles, signs, and wonders. He was known biblically as "The Tishbite," the prophet who called fire down from the heavens, and he performed at least sixteen other miracles during his tenure. Elijah was a rare breed that just showed up on the scene out of nowhere as a voice crying, "prepare ye the way of the Lord". Yet even he experienced fear and doubt.

1 Kings 19:1-9 AMP

Now Ahab told Jezebel all that Elijah had done, and how he had killed all the prophets [of Baal] with the sword. Then Jezebel sent a messenger to Elijah, saying, "So may the gods do to me, and even more, if by this time tomorrow I do not make your life like the life of one of them." And Elijah was afraid and arose and ran for his life, and he came to Beersheba which belongs to Judah, and he left his servant there. But he himself traveled a day's journey into the wilderness, and he came and sat down under a juniper tree and asked [God] that he might die. He said, "It is enough; now, O Lord, take my life, for I am no better than my fathers." He lay down and slept under the juniper tree, and behold, an angel touched him and said to him, "Get up and eat." He looked, and by his head there was a bread cake baked on hot coal, and a pitcher of water. So he ate and drank and lay down again. Then the angel of the Lord came again a second time and touched him and said, "Get up, and eat, for the journey is too long for you [without adequate sustenance]." So he got up and ate and drank, and with the strength of that food he traveled forty days and nights to Horeb (Sinai), the mountain of God.

I believe that many of you right now may be in a place like the prophet Elijah, under a Juniper tree. Things may have been going fine at one point; and then all of a sudden, something occurred unexpectedly to cause disappointment: People acting indifferently towards you, pressures of life producing natural and spiritual stress, struggles with your identity and purpose, or dealing with emotional traumas and complacency. We all contend with these physical and mental dispositions to some extent.

Elijah got word that Jezebel was after him, and he had a moment of mistaken identity. I believe that a spirit of witchcraft was at work on his behalf. Just for a moment, he allowed his feelings to move him out of faith. He forgot who he was and who his God was.

Believe me, I know what that's like. Things can happen in a moment that can shake your courage and reposition you into a fear zone or lack of clarity zone. This is the place we can often fall into if we are not cautious and attentive to what's going on in our surroundings or our circumstances.

Even though Elijah in this light was viewed by many as quitting and throwing in the towel, I want you to see the other side of his ordeal—and that was restoration.

We see the evidence in Scripture where God's hand intervened in the life of the prophet Elijah. God sends an angel to strengthen him, and he was supplied with supernatural food and water. Elijah gets up after a second time of eating, and straight off his meal makes a forty-day and forty-night journey to Horeb, the mountain of God, in **1 Kings 19:8**.

God was not done with the prophet Elijah, just as He is not done with you! There are places you still have to go and things you still have to do that are part of your destiny.

Sitting under a Juniper tree represents a disposition of quitting, backing down, a lack of courage, a loss of assignment, or allowing others to exert power over your gift and calling. At times, it is a spirit of witchcraft working behind the scenes, trying to manipulate your mantle or your mission. Witchcraft is something many believers often deal with. Simply put, it's a form of mental and spiritual warfare in the mind.

2 Corinthians 10:3-5 NIV

For though we live in the world, we do not wage war as the world does. The weapons we fight with are not the weapons of the world. On the contrary, they have divine power to demolish strongholds. We demolish arguments and every pretension that sets itself up against the knowledge of God, and we take captive every thought to make it obedient to Christ.

The word "witchcraft" occurs three times in the King James Version.

First, in **1 Samuel 15:23**, "the sin of witchcraft" could also be read as in the margin of the Revised Version, "the sin of divination". The latter represents the Hebrew word qecem, which is generally translated as "divination".

Second, the phrase that Manasseh "used witchcraft" in **2 Chronicles 33:6** is properly rendered in the Revised Version (British and American) as "practiced sorcery". The participle derived from the Hebrew verb "Kishsheph" in **Exodus 22:18** and **Deuteronomy 18:10** is translated in the King James Version as "witch".

Third, the word translated as "witchcraft" in the King James

Version in **Galatians 5:20** (Pharmakeia) is the ordinary Greek word for "sorcery". It is rendered as such in the Revised Version (British and American), although it literally means the act of administering drugs and of giving magical potions.

"Through the Doorway of error are Disorder and a Disconnection from the spirit of truth, and witchcraft is right down the hallway from it. Beware!"

The spirit of witchcraft can play a part in keeping you in the dark concerning your destiny. It can also be a contributor to trapping you in a mental state of confusion and chaos. But I want to share with you just a few simple signs that may be able to help you identify if you're under a witchcraft spell.

One of the signs of witchcraft is that vain imaginations such as fear, doubt, defeat, and failure may be tormenting you.

- A state of strong confusion.
- When you feel like often quitting.
- There is the presence of a controlling spirit like a python, causing you to feel restricted.
- Often breaking rank and isolating yourself for no apparent reason.

- Just don't want to be bothered.
- You become open to being unstable, undependable, and unfaithful.
- A strong spirit of weariness, heaviness, and fatigue sets on you.
- You become lethargic or a spirit of apathy rests on you. (In other words, you're not on the cutting edge in your worship, prayer life, reading the Word, fasting, and even your giving might be affected.)
- Lastly, a loss of spiritual identity occurs.

We discover these not only happening in the prophet Elijah's life, but several others in the Bible, and even present-day believers as well. I can recall several times in my own life when I dealt with this demon.

It attempts to manipulate your mind into thinking a way that is contrary to what the Word has said about your life. It is a very deceptive spirit intent on destroying your assignment. This occurs through the infiltration and violation of the mind. This is why we consistently need to renew our mind with the Word of God daily.

Romans 12:2 NIV

Do not conform to the pattern of this world, but be transformed by the renewing of your mind. Then you will be able to test and approve what God's will is—his good, pleasing and perfect will.

"I have come to this conclusion: God has a plan for you called 'alignment', and the Devil has a plan as well, and it's called 'misalignment.'"

"Remember whose you are and Whom you serve. Provoke yourself by recollection, and your affection for God will increase tenfold; your imagination will not be starved any longer, but will be quick and enthusiastic, and your hope will be inexpressibly bright."

- Oswald Chambers

Chapter 15

LIBRARY OF CLARITY

The Spirit of God assists with a degree of clarity for our lives. When we're in fear, we lose sight of clarity; but when there's boldness, you walk in a greater sense of clarity. I believe that the following verses relate to clarity.

Psalm 23:1-6 KJV

The Lord is my shepherd; I shall not want. He maketh me to lie down in green pastures: he leadeth me beside the still waters. He restoreth my soul: he leadeth me in the paths of righteousness for his name's sake. Yea, though I walk through the valley of the shadow of death, I will fear no evil: for thou art with me; thy rod and thy staff they comfort me. Thou preparest a table before me in the presence of mine enemies: thou anointest my head with oil; my cup runneth over. Surely goodness and mercy shall follow me all the days of my life: and I will dwell in the house of the Lord for ever.

Psalm 25:4 NIV

Show me your ways, Lord, teach me your paths.

Psalm 25:9 NIV

He guides the humble in what is right and teaches them his way.

Psalm 32:8 NIV

I will instruct you and teach you in the way you should go; I will counsel you with my loving eye on you.

Psalm 37:23 KJV

The steps of a good man are ordered by the Lord: and he delighteth in his way.

Psalm 48:14 KJV

For this God is our God for ever and ever: he will be our guide even unto death.

Psalm 119:18 NIV

Open my eyes that I may see wonderful things in your law.

Proverbs 2:6-9 NLT

For the Lord grants wisdom! From his mouth come knowledge and understanding. He grants a treasure of common sense to the honest. He is a shield to those who walk with integrity. He guards the paths of the just and protects those who are faithful to him. Then you will understand what is right, just, and fair, and you will find the right way to go.

Proverbs 16:3 NIV

Commit to the Lord whatever you do, and he will establish your plans.

Proverbs 16:9 NIV

In their hearts humans plan their course, but the Lord establishes their steps.

Proverbs 20:18 NIV

Plans are established by seeking advice; so if you wage war, obtain guidance.

Proverbs 20:24 NIV

A person's steps are directed by the Lord. How then can anyone understand their own way?

Isaiah 48:17 NIV

This is what the Lord says—your Redeemer, the Holy One of Israel: "I am the Lord your God, who teaches you what is best for you, who directs you in the way you should go.

Isaiah 58:11 NIV

The Lord will guide you always; he will satisfy your needs in a sun-scorched land and will strengthen your frame. You will be like a well-watered garden, like a spring whose waters never fail.

Matthew 7:7-8 NIV

Ask and it will be given to you; seek and you will find; knock and the door will be opened to you. For everyone who asks receives; the one who seeks finds; and to the one who knocks, the door will be opened

2 Timothy 1:7 NIV

For the Spirit God gave us does not make us timid, but gives us power, love and self-discipline.

Hebrews 4:16 KJV

Let us therefore come boldly unto the throne of grace, that we may obtain mercy, and find grace to help in time of need.

James 1:5-8 NIV

If any of you lacks wisdom, you should ask God, who gives generously to all without finding fault, and it will be given to you. But when you ask, you must believe and not doubt, because the one who doubts is like a wave of the sea, blown and tossed by the wind. That person should not expect to receive anything from the Lord. Such a person is double-minded and unstable in all they do.

"THE CROSSOVER"

"Adversity is the price that we pay for the Advancement!"

Chapter 16

PROMISED LAND

The Bible contains many passages referring to "crossing over," sometimes explicit but often implied. The first explicit crossing was when Abram crossed over the Euphrates River into Canaan to accept God's gift of the Promised Land.

Joshua 24:3 NIV
But I took your father Abraham from the land beyond the Euphrates and led him throughout Canaan and gave him many descendants.

And Moses of course, who crossed over the Red Sea, ending the enslavement of the Israelites in **Exodus Chapter 14.** These are just two of the spectacular supernatural events that occurred in biblical history.

"Desperation can be the very door that your breakthrough walks through. It can destroy or dispel the disposition of complacency."

I declare that where you are right now is not where you are going! There is an avenue with the word "access" on it; and you're about to enter into a place of grace and favor, and your life will never be the same.

The Enemy has a design to keep you imprisoned in your current state or predicament. Your faith will always be tested. As a matter of fact, you don't realize what you really have until you've been presented with a challenge.

What the Devil loves to do is try to get you to constantly and continually question the integrity of God's Word. As believers, we must know and understand that there is a crossover with your name on it, and it will require you to make a move in faith. I have an acronym that I often use for faith:

F-ull
A-ssurance
I-n
T-he
H-eart

There will always be tactics of fear (False-Evidence-Appearing-Real) and intimidation that will try to block, deter, discourage, prevent, or stop you from experiencing your crossover moment. I want to encourage you to continue to plow, push, and persevere. I have discovered in my own personal walk with God that when He speaks a prophetic word through someone or even directly to you, it's always going to require faith. That word "faith" in Hebrew is "emunah." According to Strong's reference, it states that faith is an action-oriented word. Faith implied here is basically not staying in the same condition, but moving towards your future **(2 Corinthians 13:5).**

The Hebrew root "aman" means "firm", something that is supported or secure. This word is used in **Isaiah 22:23** for a nail that is fastened to a secure place. Derived from this root is the word "emun", meaning "craftsman". A craftsman is one who is firm and secure in his talent. The feminine form of emun is the word "emunah", meaning "firmness", something or someone that is firm in their actions. When the Hebrew word "emunah" is translated as "faith", as it often is, misconceptions of its meaning occur.

Faith is usually perceived as a knowing, while the Hebrew word emunah is a firm action. To have faith in Elohim is not merely knowing that Elohim exists or knowing that He will act, rather it is that "the one with emunah will act with firmness toward Elohim's will". According to a Hebrew custom, one study states that every believer should know at least these six words here:

Hesed which denotes "love" according to **Isaiah 54:10**
Emunah which denotes "faith" according to **James 2:17**
Tefillah which denotes "prayer" according to **Luke 18:1**
Ruach which denotes "breath" according to **Genesis 2:7**
Shalom which denotes "peace" according to **John 14:25-29**
Nephesh which denotes "soul" according to **Jeremiah 6:16, Matthew 22:37, and 3 John 1:2**

I love how there are six specific words. The number "6" represents the number of men in God's number system. I believe God wants everyone related to mankind to be complete in Him through these six things.

James 2:14-26 NIV
What good is it, my brothers and sisters, if someone claims to have faith but has no deeds? Can such faith save them? Suppose a brother or a sister is without clothes and daily food. If one of you says to them, "Go in peace; keep warm and well fed," but does nothing about their physical needs, what good is it? In the same way, faith

by itself, if it is not accompanied by action, is dead.

But someone will say, "You have faith; I have deeds."

Show me your faith without deeds, and I will show you my faith by my deeds. You believe that there is one God. Good! Even the demons believe that—and shudder.

You foolish person, do you want evidence that faith without deeds is useless? Was not our father Abraham considered righteous for what he did when he offered his son Isaac on the altar? You see that his faith and his actions were working together, and his faith was made complete by what he did. And the Scripture was fulfilled that says, "Abraham believed God, and it was credited to him as righteousness," and he was called God's friend. You see that a person is considered righteous by what they do and not by faith alone.

In the same way, was not even Rahab the prostitute considered righteous for what she did when she gave lodging to the spies and sent them off in a different direction? As the body without the spirit is dead, so faith without deeds is dead.

"When you operate in the realm of faith, the invisible eventually becomes visible, and your faith converts to fruit."

We see in the life of Moses, that he was presented with a major challenge. On the one hand, he had his past in the back of his mind. On top of that, he had the crisis with the children of Israel.

Moses had to deal with constant complaining and the people disregarding him as God's prophet for the hour. Yet he still had to remain focused on his assignment as the one the Lord chose to lead the children of Israel out of the grip of the hard taskmaster, Pharaoh.

PROMISED PLAN

Some of you right now reading this book need to hear me. God has a plan for your life! You are not here to just survive, but to thrive. You are here to bless a specific person or people that the Lord has given you the grace to touch. No one else can lead worship the way you do, prophesy the way you do, preach and teach the way you do, administrate the way you do… I can go on and on here, but I believe you get the picture.

There is an old Chinese proverb that states, "When the word dangerous is presented, interpret it as an opportunity." When you are faced with a trial, I want to encourage you not to see it as "Oh my, this is the end!" But I want you to see it as, "Here is a chance for my God to show Himself strong and mighty."

Let me remind you that the God we serve always watches over His word to perform what He said He would do.

Isaiah 55:10-11 AMP

For as the rain and snow come down from heaven, and do not return there without watering the earth, making it bear and sprout, and providing seed to the sower and bread to the eater, so will My word be which goes out of My mouth; it will not return to Me void (useless, without result), without accomplishing what I desire and without succeeding in the matter for which I sent it.

Jeremiah 1:12 NIV

The Lord said to me, "You have seen correctly, for I am watching to see that my word is fulfilled."

"When your life is on course with its purpose, you are your most powerful."

- Oprah Winfrey

"You were seeded into this generation by God to produce what no one else could. So own it, and watch the harvest grow."

People will always be people, in the sense that they will sometimes try to bring you to a place of discouragement. When in actuality, perhaps you've awakened the insecurity or laziness they possess. People will be saying things like, "You can't do this; you'll never make it out of this situation." We see this insecurity evident in the Old Testament, in the life of King Saul.

Please hear me when I say this. You are equipped for more than you realize. There is untapped potential present in you that will awaken and activate when you get around the right people.

Moses struggled with insecurities. It has been stated by biblical scholars that Moses had a speech impediment. But in spite of all of the things he encountered, he had to believe that God is, and will always be, faithful concerning His Word.

"When you develop a sense of security in your calling, often times it awakens insecurities and indifference in others. You need to remain focused and fixed on His face and not the face of others."

Philippians 3:14 AMP

I press on toward the goal to win the [heavenly] prize of the upward call of God in Christ Jesus.

Exodus 3:7-12 AMP

The LORD said, "I have in fact seen the affliction (suffering, desolation) of my people who are in Egypt, and have heard their cry because of their taskmasters (oppressors); for I know their pain and suffering. So I have come down to rescue them from the hand (power) of the Egyptians, and to bring them up from that land to a land [that is] good and spacious, to a land flowing with milk and honey [a land of plenty]—to the place of the Canaanite, the Hittite, the Amorite, the Perizzite, the Hivite, and the Jebusite.

"Now, behold, the cry of the children of Israel has come to me; and I have also seen how the Egyptians oppress them. Therefore, come now, and I will send you to Pharaoh, and then bring my people, the children of Israel, out of Egypt."

But Moses said to God, "Who am I, that I should go to Pharaoh, and that I should bring the children of Israel out of Egypt?" And God said, "Certainly I will be with you, and this shall be the sign to you that it is I who have sent you: when you have brought the people out of Egypt, you shall serve and worship God at this mountain."

"When God favors you, what is meant to break you will propel you towards a breakthrough because the seed of breakthrough has been planted in you, and now it's time to release it to grow."

Chapter 17

BREAKING THE SPIRIT OF PHARAOH

Before we get into this subject, let's look at a little background history of a pharaoh. I have discovered that sometimes, the best way to know a thing is to be able to gauge or make a connection to its past. So, let's journey into the nature or the inception of a pharaoh, the ancient Egyptian rulers.

Because of its long history, ancient Egypt had many, many pharaohs. The ancient Egyptian empire lasted from about 3150 BC to about 31 BC. You can figure out how long that is by doing a simple subtraction problem. Throughout that time, there were about 170 pharaohs in all. Most Egyptologists (people who study ancient Egypt) believe that Narmer was the first pharaoh of Egypt, but they know that Cleopatra VII was the last.

Pharaohs were known as the Lord and High Priest over two lands, the upper and lower parts of their respected areas in Egypt. They owned all of the land in Egypt, enacted laws, collected taxes, and defended Egypt from invaders as the commander-in-chief of the army.

Yet another role of the pharaoh was as an intermediary between the deities and the people. They deputized for the deities in the roles as both a civil and religious administrator. In Egyptian society, religion was central to everyday life. Religiously, the pharaoh officiated over religious ceremonies and chose the sites of new temples.

The pharaoh was also responsible for maintaining Maat, or cosmic order, balance, and justice. Part of this included going to war when necessary to defend the country or attacking others when it was believed it would contribute to Maat, such as to obtain resources.

Some more interesting facts about a pharaoh of Egypt:

Pharaohs would wear a striped headcloth (called Nemes) that would cover the entire crown (called a Uraeus), the back of their head, and the nape of their neck. The Nemes had two large flaps which hung down behind the ears and in front of both shoulders (Wikipedia). If you notice, the top of their head looked like a cobra. The Uraeus (the pharaoh's crown) was an upright cobra! The earliest evidence known of the Uraeus as a rearing cobra was from the reign of Den, in the First Dynasty. It signified that the pharaoh was ready to strike their enemies with venom at any time. The cobra supposedly protected the pharaoh by spitting fire at its enemies.

Have you ever noticed that in depictions of pharaohs, they always have a beard? This is called a false beard. In real life, most Egyptian men were clean-shaven; but pharaohs, even the female ones, wore false beards that they tied on. Usually, the beards were plaited like a big braid. No one is really sure why the ancient Egyptian pharaohs did this. Since some of their gods had beards, perhaps the pharaohs thought it connected them more closely to the gods.

A pharaoh's personality was also unlike any other of their time. We've seen them in movies portrayed a certain way—but there is always more than meets the eye. I want to help bring a little more clarity as it relates to the disposition that a pharaoh possessed. From what we've gathered through history, it appears as though each pharaoh had a distinctive nature, but what connected them all was the fact that they were taught and trained to dictate and rule. Politics were in their blood. They had to learn the laws of the land and the codes for ruling a kingdom.

Many pharaohs went to war when their land was threatened or when they wanted to control foreign lands. If the pharaoh won the battle, the conquered people had to recognize the Egyptian pharaoh as their ruler and offer him the finest and most valuable goods of their land. With that in mind, let's explore the Spirit of Pharaoh for just a couple of moments.

The Spirit of Pharaoh is an anti-progress spirit that works hard to limit or stop growth. It wants to limit or stop your creativity, mobility, and productivity. This spirit wants to govern and guide your movements and wants to infuse and influence your decision-making faculties. It is a spirit that will sit on you with the intent to get everything out of you for its own benefit only and not yours. The Spirit of Pharaoh is an oppressive spirit that breeds contempt and depression.

This Spirit of Pharaoh is a domineering spirit, it is a demanding spirit, it is a destructive spirit, it is a disruptive spirit, it is a dismantling spirit, it is a dividing spirit, it is a desensitized spirit, it is a deceptive spirit, and lastly, it is a demonic spirit.

★★★

CHARACTERISTICS OF THE SPIRIT OF PHARAOH

1. The Spirit of Pharaoh distracts us from our true purpose.

God said in **Jeremiah 1:5 NIV**

"Before I formed you in the womb I knew you, before you were born I set you apart; I appointed you as a prophet to the nations."

Ephesians 1:4 NIV

For he chose us in him before the creation of the world to be holy and blameless in his sight. In love he predestined us for adoption to sonship through Jesus Christ, in accordance with his pleasure and will—to the praise of his glorious grace, which he has freely given us in the One he loves.

"Every one of God's children is born with a divine purpose. This purpose trumps our personal plans for ourselves and guarantees a fulfilled life."

Moses had a distraction in the course of fulfilling his purpose when he killed an Egyptian man. Consequently, he had to flee from Pharaoh to a foreign land (recall **Exodus 2:11-15**). But eventually, God called him back, armed him spiritually, and sent him once again to Egypt. In the same vein, God directs and redirects the path of His children to their destinies—if we would only trust Him.

2. *The Spirit of Pharaoh confuses our identity.*

We live in an age when too many people are unsure of their identities; many don't know their worth. Moses himself lived for many years with dual identities: One as an Israelite slave and another as the son of the princess of Egypt. But God knew who he truly was because God had chosen him. The Bible lets us know that God has good plans towards us.

Jeremiah 29:11-14 NIV

"For I know the plans I have for you," declares the Lord, "plans to prosper you and not to harm you, plans to give you hope and a future. Then you will call on me and come and pray to me, and I will listen to you. You will seek me and find me when you seek me with all your heart. I will be found by you," declares the Lord, "and will bring you back from captivity. I will gather you from all the nations and places where I have banished you," declares the Lord,

"and will bring you back to the place from which I carried you into exile."

So when we live in His Word, we don't have any doubts about who we are. Our identity is not in the world, but in Christ Jesus.

3. The Spirit of Pharaoh fights the next generation.

Pharaoh had ordered the massacre of all Hebrew baby boys because he feared they would grow to become powerful and fight against him. In the same way, the Spirit of Pharaoh fights the next generation. God promised to pour out His Spirit upon all flesh in the last days, causing supernatural manifestations in the form of dreams and visions.

Joel 2:28 NIV

And afterward, I will pour out my Spirit on all people.
Your sons and daughters will prophesy, your old men will dream dreams, your young men will see visions.

Hence, acceleration and groundbreaking success is assured for God's people.

4. The Spirit of Pharaoh hardens our hearts.

Pharaoh's heart was hardened against God, and he refused to carry out His will to let the Israelites go. This disobedience ultimately cost him his life. Disobedience to God is a sin and prevents us from being partakers in His divine blessings.

If we love God, we will obey His Word and keep His commandments.

John 14:15 NIV

"If you love me, keep my commands."

5. The Spirit of Pharaoh will pursue one last time.

After finally allowing the Israelites to leave Egypt, Pharaoh changed his mind against them. He took his army and charged after the Israelites one last time and met a watery end at the bottom of the Red Sea.

Exodus 14:23-28 NIV

The Egyptians pursued them, and all Pharaoh's horses and chariots and horsemen followed them into the sea. During the last watch of the night the Lord looked down from the pillar of fire and cloud at the Egyptian army and threw it into confusion. He jammed the wheels of their chariots so that they had difficulty driving. And the Egyptians said, "Let's get away from the Israelites! The Lord is fighting for them against Egypt."

Then the Lord said to Moses, "Stretch out your hand over the sea so that the waters may flow back over the Egyptians and their chariots and horsemen." Moses stretched out his hand over the sea, and at daybreak the sea went back to its place. The Egyptians were fleeing toward it, and the Lord swept them into the sea. The water flowed back and covered the chariots and horsemen—the entire army of Pharaoh that had followed the Israelites into the sea. Not one of them survived.

The Devil and his cohorts are hell-bent on taking out the children of God and will keep attempting to do so. Therefore, you must have a deep relationship with God, and be grounded in His word to remain unshakable when they strike.

There are several ways to deal with these spirits, including: creating an environment of praise and worship, spending quality time in the Word until you catch a revelation, going through a form of deliverance, receiving a prophetic word from the Lord through your man or woman of God which will instantaneously set you free, and acquainting yourself more with the Holy Spirit.

Whichever route you choose to go, sometimes, you may have to smash it down (literally) like the Hulk from Marvel, until it breaks off of you. This is a spirit that always tries to pursue/control, limit/restrict, and stop you from spending time with God.

To defeat your Pharaoh, you must understand what he does. There is no need to be negotiating with evil spirits. The only language they understand is violence through authority.

Matthew 11:12 NIV

From the days of John the Baptist until now, the kingdom of heaven has been subjected to violence, and violent people have been raiding it.

★★★

HOLY, ACCEPTABLE

The following excerpt is taken from multiplyingfreedom.com:

The only language the Spirit of Pharaoh will understand is the language of signs, wonders, fire, and power, demonstrated in the Spirit of God. The glory of God is the greatest instrument for defeating your Pharaoh. Strive to stay in the presence of the Lord until you are filled with His glory, and walk in the realm that can bring defeat to this spirit. To bring him down, you must:

1) Eat the Passover covenant meal (Jesus is the Passover Lamb – you must be saved); you need to undertake the mystery of libation to ease your way out of Egypt. In other words, do your due diligence with Holy Communion **(1 Corinthian 11:27-34)**.

2) The blood must be on the lintel of your life (you are the house of God); you must sprinkle the blood all over you, your loved ones, and everything that is around you **(Exodus 12:13-15)**.

3) It is important to have someone that can hear from God in the

event that you are under the control of a principality or spirit that has you trapped in a certain state of life, like Pharaoh did with the children of Israel. Follow the instruction and leadership of the Lord through the man of God, your prophet. Who is your Moses? **(Romans 13:1-2)**.

4) You must persevere and pray without ceasing: this spirit is very stubborn **(1 Thessalonians 5:16-18)**.

5) When you obey the Lord, allow Him to fight for you. If you fight Pharaoh alone, you will lose the battle. Do it by instruction. Just as Moses directed the children of Israel, so is your prophet to direct you out of the bondage of your Egypt through divine instruction. The battle is the Lord's! **(2 Chronicles 20:15)**.

6) Release plagues against Pharaoh as you plead the Blood of Jesus **(1 Peter 1:18-19)**. You may not know what is occurring in the spirit realm (the Spirit of Pharaoh will pretend like nothing is happening); but, Pharaoh was getting weaker and weaker as Moses, by the Spirit of the Lord, released plagues against Egypt.

7) Expect a last-minute miracle of deliverance after the fight of faith. Abraham and Sarah weren't expecting what God did for

them, even though He told them what He was about to do **(Genesis 21:1-7)**.

Another thing Pharaoh did was afflict God's people with hard labor and made them build his cities. This clearly depicts secular work today. People work hard in their secular jobs but give little or no service at all to the house of God. We spend almost all our time and energy on things that have nothing to do with God's work, without realizing that we are indirectly working for Pharaoh. We need to be very cautious not to allow things, people, or situations replace or substitute God. You can easily fall into this mode and not even realize it at times.

I get the fact that you want to make sure your family needs are met. I get the fact you want nice things in life; but at the cost of your relationship with God? It's not worth it! So many believers stumble and fall into this trap. In doing so, they become more and more distant from spiritual things. Many churches have fallen victim to this spirit. Remember, this Spirit of Pharaoh will make every attempt to keep you employed under its system and not God's system.

For some of us, it may be a trust or heart issue. But at the end of the day, you can't serve two masters **(Matthew 6:24)**. The Spirit of Pharaoh would love nothing more than to keep you under its hold and influence. I want to encourage you wherever you are in life, trust Him.

Exodus 1:8–13 NIV

Then a new king, to whom Joseph meant nothing, came to power in Egypt. "Look," he said to his people, "the Israelites have become far too numerous for us. Come, we must deal shrewdly with them or they will become even more numerous and, if war breaks out, will join our enemies, fight against us and leave the country." So they put slave masters over them to oppress them with forced labor, and they built Pithom and Rameses as store cities for Pharaoh. But the more they were oppressed, the more they multiplied and spread; so the Egyptians came to dread the Israelites and worked them ruthlessly. They made their lives bitter with harsh labor in brick and mortar and with all kinds of work in the fields; in all their harsh labor the Egyptians worked them ruthlessly.

★★★

A TYPE AND FORESHADOW

"Pharaoh is a 'type' of Satan. Egypt is a 'type' of the world, and Israel is a 'type' of God's people."

Egypt was a place during Pharaoh's reign where you did not want to set up camp. It was a place where Pharaoh was the dictator, and you, as a slave, had no say. Being enslaved to something or someone is never a good state to be in. They determine your life; they determine what you eat and where you go, among other things. You literally have no voice and are very limited in your form of expression.

I couldn't imagine the discontent and disdain that the children of Israel must have struggled with. Some of you right now may be in a situation where you are dealing with similar issues, whether it is a job, your ministry, or business related. In that particular place, there might be an overbearing, domineering, insensitive, controlling, manipulative display that belittles you, all or most of the time. Pharaoh did this to the children of Israel. He forced them to internally and mentally suppress who they really were as human beings. He had them adapt to a complacent disposition and surrender their identities in silence.

This very same spirit tried to kill Moses as a baby in order to stop him from fulfilling his purpose. But God spared and delivered him, just like God would save Jesus as a baby from the Spirit of Herod many centuries later. I know many of us can relate to these scenarios. The Enemy has made several attempts, time after time, to destroy you. There may even be some of you who are parents that have contemplated having an abortion because of current pressures and circumstances.

Do you know that there are nearly 1,000,000 abortions per year on average? Those are just the ones that have been reported, there are probably so many others that we may not even be aware of. Think about all of the potential world-changers and innovators that never got a chance to present themselves, their talents, or their gifts on the stage of this world as we know it.

In situations like these, we can see the Spirit of Pharaoh playing a role. This spirit is like the Terminator, in the sense that it wants to annihilate the bloodline and the birth of the first-born male seed. This same spirit still roams the earth today in a quest to keep the children of God in repression, digression, depression, suppression, and oppression.

Pharaoh's name denotes "destroyer". It is a strongman—a principal spirit—controlling a person, family, place, or thing and holding them in bondage. It tries to curtail your spiritual, physical, financial, marital, and any other freedom that will enable you to live your full potential for the Lord. I declare it has robbed us of our godly inheritance long enough. It's time for a change!

So many Christians don't realize how this spirit is often present in their lives. This is why I believe that wherever you are right now, it's not God's best for you. There is so much more He has in store for you. The Spirit of Pharaoh has had its way for too long in the lives of many believers. You have to make a decision today to lead the charge as Moses did, and exit your Egypt.

The children of Israel may have been in bondage for over 400 years, but you don't have to be in bondage for any length of time. Whoever your Pharaoh is, don't let him (or it) bluff you, play you, or punk you any longer into believing you have no right to rise up, or that life cannot be any different than what has always been. As I often say, "the Devil is a liar and his mother-in-law too!" Jesus came to release us all from the tyranny, the terror, the torment, and the tongue of Pharaoh!

I want to just decree and declare right here that God is indeed raising up a Moses for this generation. One that will contest, defy, and destroy the Spirit of Pharaoh. This is definitely one spirit that the Body of Christ has been assaulted by for some time, and it has become more and more prevalent.

So many Christians around the world are under some spiritual attack or assault to some degree. Unfortunately, many of them don't have an answer or can't identify the principality they are up against. This is one particular spirit that the Lord has had me focus on over the last couple months now.

I know of so many relatives, friends, colleagues, and associates that were on the verge of a crossover, but then it happened! Out of nowhere, something unexplainable began to manifest and occur.

I have learned over the years that the Devil doesn't want to let you go. But I hear it resounding loud in my spirit right now, "Tell Pharaoh to let you go! Let your family go! Let your ministry go! Let your business go! Let your job go! Let your health go! Let your marriage go! Let your mind go!"

Open up your mouth, and declare it right now. You stand from a place of authority. The victory is yours now, in Jesus' name. Come on, right now, wherever you are, take authority, and never forget Whose you are.

How many of you right now are so tired of never really advancing? Well, I have great news for you. Extra, extra, read all about it!!! God did it before, and He's about to do it again for you and your house. Glory to God!

Hebrews 13:8 TPT

Jesus, the Anointed One, is always the same—yesterday, today, and forever.

Chapter 18

PRAYER FOR AUTHORITY

I want you all to pray this quick prayer with me right now.

"Lord of angel armies, the great I AM, and mighty in battle, the Bible says that I can decree a thing, and it shall be established.

I cancel and nullify any curses that were spoken over us intentionally or unintentionally.

I cancel the effects of those negative words over my family and future generations.

I declare and decree that generational curses of sickness, poverty, marital failure, bareness, rage, alcoholism, and lying are null and void. They will never manifest because we are free from them.

I command the Devil and his demons, Pharaoh, and every settling spirit, to leave my family alone.

Spirit of oppression and depression I no longer accept you in my mind. You are now evicted, in the name of Jesus. This spirit can no longer hold on to my destiny and my greatness.

I issue out a death warrant on this Spirit of Pharaoh. May every grip it has had be burned by the fire of the Holy Ghost.

I am ready Lord to walk in my Canaan land now, in Jesus' name!"

✵✵✵

BE ALERT!

"Oftentimes, it is the pain of being you that creates and taps in to the power of being you."

I want to declare over you a new yielding season in God. Many of you have approached the door of deliverance, but have been accustomed to being in a state of defeat. It's like the lack of passion to push is present. Child of God, you are so close to crossing over your Red Sea.

How do I know this, you ask?

Let me just say that when you are on the verge of a major victory, several unusual things occur:

Indifference and insecurity are amplified.

The opposition begins to intensify.

Old mindsets will start warring with the new.

Pharaoh will make every attempt to get you to quit.

All of a sudden, after these things occur, doors start opening up that you could have never imagined.

Chapter 19

HIS WEIGHT IN THE WIND

In **Exodus 14:21**, we discover a massive move of God that happened in the life of Moses. He was given a specific instruction that I can only imagine in the natural mind wouldn't make sense. But when it comes to faith, God may never give details or require your understanding. He will, however, require your obedience!

The Bible said that as a result of Moses stretching out his hand over the Red Sea, a strong east wind came through where they were standing and blew the waters back to the degree that there was dry land for them to cross over. This is one story that fascinates me and builds up my faith, as I pray it will for you as well.

We see in this encounter what I want to call "His weight in the wind". There is so much power in the God we serve. We see this validated in the life of Moses and the children of Israel. In the weight of His wind is His authority, His dominion, His greatness, His favor, His power, His glory, and His nature.

Through science, we see the wind carries with it what is called "cause and effect". There are things that contribute to wind and then there are the results or effects of it.

Scripture describes the powerful effect of wind and uses the image figuratively to speak of God's power and presence in the world.

The Greek word for spirit, "pneuma" (Strong's 4151) has a similar meaning to the Hebrew word "ruach". "Pneuma": to breathe or blow, primarily denotes the wind.

The word for "spirit" (rucha, ruach) in Aramaic and Hebrew can denote "breath", "wind", or "spirit".

John 3:8 NIV
"The wind blows wherever it pleases. You hear its sound, but you cannot tell where it comes from or where it is going. So it is with everyone born of the Spirit."

The Bible also references the wind in the four directions: north, south, east, and west. The four winds in the Bible are the power of God in the natural world, basically where "miracles" can occur and where the strength of God is made visible to humans.

The Prophet Daniel saw a vision by night.

Daniel 7:2-3 (paraphrased)

"Behold, the four winds of the sky broke out on the great sea. Four great animals came up from the sea, diverse one from another."

The Prophet Zechariah saw four chariots rise up between two mountains and asked an angel what these were.

Zechariah 6:5 (paraphrased)

The angel answered: "These are the four winds of the sky, which go out from standing before the Lord of all the earth."

God uses the Four Winds to breathe life into skeletons to create a great army in **Ezekiel 37:9**.

The Four Winds also carry God's chosen people to their destiny, both in the Old Testament **(Exodus 14:21)** and in the New Testament:

Matthew 24:31 (paraphrased)

"He will send out his angels with a great sound of a trumpet, and they will gather together his chosen ones from the four winds, from

one end of the sky to the other."

Here are several more Scriptures I'd like to share with the reference of God in the wind and using it for His purpose:

2 Samuel 22:11 NIV

He mounted the cherubim and flew; he soared on the wings of the wind.

Psalms 104:2-4 NIV

The Lord wraps himself in light as with a garment; he stretches out the heavens like a tent and lays the beams of his upper chambers on their waters.

He makes the clouds his chariot and rides on the wings of the wind.

He makes winds his messengers, flames of fire his servants.

Nahum 1:3 NIV

The Lord is slow to anger but great in power; the Lord will not leave the guilty unpunished. His way is in the whirlwind and the storm.

Isaiah 59:19 AMP

So they will fear the name of the Lord from the west, and His glory from the rising of the sun. For He will come in like a narrow, rushing stream which the breath of the Lord drives [overwhelming the Enemy].

Acts 2:1-4 AMP

When the day of Pentecost had come, they were all together in one place, and suddenly a sound came from heaven like a rushing violent wind, and it filled the whole house where they were sitting. There appeared to them tongues resembling fire, which were being distributed [among them], and they rested on each one of them [as each person received the Holy Spirit]. And they were all filled [that is, diffused throughout their being] with the Holy Spirit and began to speak in other tongues (different languages), as the Spirit was giving them the ability to speak out [clearly and appropriately].

★★★

LEAN ON ME

We can see even in our storyline of Moses in Exodus that he had to learn how to lean on and trust God. He came in contact with the other side of God where the supernatural is the norm.

I have learned that as you lean on God, He will load you daily.

As you lean on God, He will Lead you.
As you lean on God, He will Level your field.
As you lean on God, He will bring your enemies Low.
As you lean on God, He will break the Levees of Lack.
As you lean on God, He will extend your Life.
As you lean on God, He will see to it that you have a Legacy for your Loved ones.

When we continue to lean on and trust in Him, He favors us! The favor of the Lord is dispensed as He sees fit. When something supernaturally occurs, and you couldn't have paid or worked for it, it's literally the hand of God moving in an unfavorable situation.

✷✷✷

FAVORABLE CONDITIONS

Let's have a faith building exercise here and see some of the patriarchs and matriarchs of the Bible who encountered the favor of God and others.

Abel found favor with the Lord as he offered up acceptable sacrifices **(Genesis 4:4)**.

Noah found favor when the flood came, and his family was spared **(Genesis 7:1 & 23** and **8:1-13)**.

Abram found favor in the Lord's sight and received a name change to Abraham **(Genesis 17:1-5)**.

Joseph found favor within Potiphar's house **(Genesis 39:2-4)**.

Moses found favor at the Red Sea **(Exodus 14:10-31)**.

Rahab the harlot asked God to save her despite her past **(Joshua 2:3-16)**.

Joshua found favor at the river of Jordan **(Joshua 3:1-17)**.

Samson encountered the favor of the Lord as he used the jawbone of a donkey to kill a thousand men **(Judges 15:9-17)**.

Esther found favor with King Xerxes **(Esther 2:17)**.

The prophet Elijah found favor with a widow from Zarephath and through her, he received food for his journey **(I Kings 17:7-16)**.

The one hundred prophets of God received the favor of the Lord as the prophet Obadiah gets wind of Jezebel's plan to kill the prophets. So, he hides fifty of them in one cave and fifty in another **(1 Kings 18:3-4)**.

God used the prophet Elisha in both the birthing of and the raising up of the Shunamite woman's son from the dead. She received favor from the Lord **(2 Kings 4:16-38)**.

The three Hebrew boys that were thrown in the fiery furnace found the favor of the Lord. They came out without the smell of smoke or even one burn mark on their bodies **(Daniel 3:15-27)**.

The prophet Daniel found favor in the Lion's den where the Lord shut the mouths of the lions **(Daniel 6:16-23)**.

Mary, the mother of Jesus, found the favor of the Lord when she was specifically chosen to birth the Messiah **(Luke 1:28-31)**.

Peter finds the favor of the Lord through a revelation **(Matthew 16:17-19)**.

Jesus Christ, the son of God, found favor with both God and man **(Luke 2:52)**.

Cornelius encountered the favor of the Lord in his house **(Acts 10:1-4)**.

The Apostle Paul and Silas encountered the favor of the Lord when the prison door swung open **(Acts 16:25-34)**.

I wanted to share these examples for the purpose of information, edification, exhortation, and comfort. I believe that faith really does come by what we hear, as it says in **Romans 10:17**.

Chapter 20

HIS STRONG HAND

"God will always give you an instruction prior to your Crossover."

Exodus 3:16-21 NIV

"Go, assemble the elders of Israel and say to them, 'The Lord, the God of your fathers—the God of Abraham, Isaac and Jacob—appeared to me and said: I have watched over you and have seen what has been done to you in Egypt. And I have promised to bring you up out of your misery in Egypt into the land of the Canaanites, Hittites, Amorites, Perizzites, Hivites and Jebusites—a land flowing with milk and honey.'

"The elders of Israel will listen to you. Then you and the elders are to go to the king of Egypt and say to him, 'The Lord, the God of the Hebrews, has met with us. Let us take a three-day journey into the wilderness to offer sacrifices to the Lord our God.'

"But I know that the king of Egypt will not let you go unless a mighty hand compels him. So I will stretch out my hand and strike the Egyptians with all the wonders that I will perform among them. After that, he will let you go.

"And I will make the Egyptians favorably disposed toward this people, so that when you leave you will not go empty-handed."

As we see here in this text, there was a situation that the children of Israel were in. They were being oppressed by Pharaoh. For over 400 years, they had been under a principality that would not let them go. Pharaoh had been forcing them to work day and night against their will. He was using them specifically for his benefit and self-gain.

I believe that in this amazing story of the prophet Moses, there were Trials, there were Tests, there was Torment; but God turned them into Triumph for His people. All through the life of Moses, the hand of God was there with him—in the shadows, if you will.

Moses of course had a name that carried great weight and significance. If you follow the thread of his life, his name denotes "being drawn out of." Many of you reading this book right now have been trying your whole life to figure out "what God?" or "why God?" "I don't know if I'm ready for this God." "I'm not qualified enough." "I don't have a degree or have very limited education." "They may not like what I have to say, especially as a minister of the Gospel."

Many of us have had similar questions to these, as I am sure the prophet Moses did. Every time I think about this story, I get excited and inspired all over again. If God did it then, and since He is no respecter of persons **(Acts 10:34)**, He can do it now, if He so chooses. I want you to see how relevant this story is to us now. He is still omnipresent, omnipotent, and omniscient. He is the Alpha and the Omega, the Creator of all things.

Now let's unpack these few verses in **Exodus 3** because so much power and life and faith were on display here. We cannot permit fear to occupy us in the present and keep us from pursuing after our future.

For those of you that are reading this now, I am talking exactly to you. There may have been a Pharaoh that you have been up against, and it may have refused to let you go; but I declare again, it's time to cross over.

If you notice in **Verse 16**, there was a command to go and not stay, gather the leaders (the influencers, as we would call them), and assemble together. I want to share something with you about this. I believe this was strategic because even as pastors, we know that there are certain times and moments when we must first connect with the leaders in our churches. Whether to mobilize, equip, or position them for what lies ahead or just our next action steps in reference to the vision of the house.

We see here how the Lord is giving specific instructions to Moses and the children of Israel. He's also reminding them that "I AM that I AM", "the God of Abraham, Isaac, and Jacob". I have not been ignorant or unaware of the hold that Pharaoh has on you. So, here's what I will do for you, just because you are my children.

The Lord begins to assure them, "I am concerned about the stress you're under". How many of us can relate to this right here? Can I tell you that God is concerned about your assignment, your family, your ministry, your church, your job, your business, your health, and your welfare? He's so in love with you and hasn't forgotten about you.

★★★

HE KNOWS, HE CARES

I don't know who this is for? God is and has always been concerned about you, and you have definitely been on His mind. This is why whatever has been holding you down and back is about to break. The very thing that's been in your bloodline for generations, stops today!

God is speaking to someone right now, "I am about to bring you up and out." For those of you who have been suffering financially, emotionally, mentally, and spiritually, the God that we now serve is about to move on your behalf, just because.

I declare right now a "just because grace" is about to hit your life, and you'll never be the same, in Jesus' name!

In the text here, we see how Egypt was a place of bondage and fear. It was a place that was not conducive to His people's calling. That's a word for someone right now. You're in that place as well. A place where it's not conducive to your calling.

I remember being in a ministry where I was serving in another department just to occupy or fill a position. But in my heart, I always knew there was something more God wanted me to do. I have learned over the years to trust God and always honor Him, even if it's not reciprocated.

God knows how to pull you out of that place and plant you elsewhere, so you can go and be celebrated, not just tolerated. This happens so much in the Body of Christ. Many believers get stuck or trapped in a spiritual drought. There's no moisture, no movement, no momentum when it comes to their assignments and giftings.

I can relate to this as well. But just as I have crossed over in certain areas, so can you. If you need to put on your spiritual life jacket, then so be it; but you've got to get going. Don't be like the man on the porch of Bethesda in the Bible who just made one excuse after another. Roll, if you have to. Just get there! Miracles only respond to motion that is accompanied by faith.

I have discovered over the years that there is absolutely nothing wrong with God and His Word. We've all had moments where, in some areas, there was faith; and then in others, there wasn't. The reality is that it's not really anybody else's fault that you haven't experienced the promises of God. Not the fathers of faith, not your spiritual mother, not your spiritual father. Perhaps the deficiency is with your hearing.

Oftentimes, when your hearing becomes inconsistent, you go to see the ear doctor. In most instances, they may conclude that your hearing is blocked because your ears are clogged. Your eardrum may be damaged for any number of reasons. Or some other intricate component of the ear may have been impacted over time. The bottom-line here is that your hearing plays an important role in your movement from one place to another. It affects your way of speech and communication.

Romans 10:17 NIV

Consequently, faith comes from hearing the message, and the message is heard through the word about Christ.

So many Christians miss out on crossing over into the Promise Land or the blessing of the Lord. Some get close and run out of gas and can't move anymore. People set goals and make plans all the time—but the ones who possess the prize are the ones who never quit. These are the ones who get back up after being knocked down, continue to preach even if people don't respond, and love and forgive others even if they've been wronged. They make a bridge or bust a hole in the wall to continue their progress.

You don't have to sit around and witness everyone else being blessed when you can partake as well. Think of all these great men and women of faith. Even in the secular market, they all have something in common, and it is… they never quit.

Hebrews 11:13 NIV

All these people were still living by faith when they died. They did not receive the things promised; they only saw them and welcomed them from a distance, admitting that they were foreigners and strangers on earth.

✯✯✯

BELIEVE IT, AND RECEIVE IT

I want every last one of you that are holding this book in your hands to make it, to prosper, and to cross over to the other side of better. I believe that someone reading this right now needed to hear this little dissertation on faith to receive their promise.

Now allow me to jump back into my text from **Exodus 3:17**. God begins to encourage Moses and the children of Israel that He was about to bring them into a land that is flowing, fluent, and flourishing; not broke, not defeated, not depleted, not stressed; a land that's flowing with milk and honey. Please hear me, child of God. The land you're standing on now is not God's absolute best for you.

God spoke to me last month and said, "John, I'm going to give you more than you've asked for." Hallelujah! I have been declaring this word regularly now. You can always see better results when your mouth becomes congruent to His Word and plans for your life.

God knew that Pharaoh would contest His instructions to let the people of God go; so, God began to implement His strong hand.

Now this is the word for the coming year that the Lord shared with me specifically at the start of the Jewish New Year, Rosh Hashanah. He said that this would be a year we see His strong hand move mightily on all of our affairs, and that this year would far supersede any years prior. Get ready, people of God. It's about to happen for you in so many ways, doors swinging open, and opportunities out of nowhere that will make your head spin.

Repeat this with me, "This is my year to cross over to the better in every area of my life." God says, "Get ready! Because I'm about to reach out My strong hand in this year with signs, miracles, and wonders that will get the attention of the news sector, your family, your friends, and especially your enemies." God will even let them live long enough to witness His strong hand moving supernaturally in your life.

Lastly, as I often say, "it gets gooderer and gooderer", the Lord says, "I will restore back unto your marriage, your family, your ministry, your business, your job, your name, and watch this, favor and respect. Yes, child of God. I said it—a greater level of favor and respect is about to fall on your life, just as in **Verse 21 of Exodus 3**. I pray you're ready to receive because the time has come. Yes, the set time to favor you!"

Psalms 102:13 NIV

You will arise and have compassion on Zion, for it is time to show favor to her; the appointed time has come.

The Lord also reminded me of two other words He spoke to me recently about what will begin to manifest in the lives of believers this year. One of them is "promise" and the other is "great possessions." He also shared with me that this will be the year where "I will answer your request and make good on my promises. In addition to that, I will get the attention of those who have opposed you, as I did with my servant Moses."

In this word "promise", the Lord revealed to me that there are four things that will be birthed out in the coming year:

1. Plunder

2. Power

3. Purpose

4. Position

Let's define this word "plunder" for a second because I really want you to see that there's something so different and powerful about this year. There's something that's shifting and forming in the vein of favor for the sons and daughters of God. The Bible says, "In all your getting, get understanding" **(Proverbs 4:7)**. Let's not miss this Vein of Victory that will position us with a greater Vantage point!

I declare "the greater" is on the way for you and your house. Look for the new house, look for the new car, start the business plan, and expect the investors to show up, expect debt cancellations on debts that you've had for years, and expect restoration and restitution of all things.

You have lost too much! Get ready for great possessions from the north, south, east, and west. Get ready for people to walk up to you and write you checks that you could've never imagined. Get ready to meet the right people at the right time that will cause everything you've been praying about and believing God for to come and overtake you this year.

There are some spectacular things that are about to come down the pipeline of heaven and no demonic principality, such as: Leviathan, Jezebel, Python, or any other form of witchcraft can stop what God has deemed blessed.

"What is the Spirit of Python?" you may ask. In **Acts Chapter 16**, Paul is confronted by a woman possessed with a "spirit of divination." The Greek word for divination is "python." The Spirit of Python grabs hold of you and attempts to squeeze the breath out of you spiritually. Those who believe in a Python Spirit point to **Acts 16:16**, where Scripture refers to a slave girl who had "a spirit of divination." The Greek term for "divination" in this verse is pythōna. The only way to break its grip is with a sacrifice of praise and the blood of Jesus Christ.

Remember, the Devil tried to defeat and discourage Daniel when he was praying in the **Daniel 10:2**. The thing we must realize is, if you aren't doing much, chances are, there may not be much opposition. However, when you start deciding to make a move or advance in the things of God, there will be many adversaries.

You never need to think for a second that you are the only one who has encountered something of that magnitude though. We see similar stories documented throughout the Bible where men and women of God were attacked, tested, or opposed by the

Enemy. Just learn how to shift your perspective and deflect it with the Word, with your worship and with prayer and fasting. The Greater One resides on the inside of you! Again, I declare that some amazing and astounding things are on the way.

My wife has been standing on this word that the Lord spoke to her during her time of prayer. It was, "Get ready for some amazing things. Do not quit. You're almost there!"

To those of you who feel like you're in a stage of life where some things were never supposed to happen, some jobs, some people, some relationships, believe me, I have tried to make certain things happen concerning my own life. For instance, trying to connect with certain individuals, trying to get them to notice me, trying to fit in somewhere I wasn't designed to be. If anybody gets this, I do. I believe we have all been in this place before. Perhaps some of you may even be in this place right now. It's not really a bad thing to look for affirmation, but don't base your gift or purpose of living solely on the acceptance and opinions of others. It's a trap door to disappointment, rejection, and depression.

Matthew 6:1-4 NIV

"Be careful not to practice your righteousness in front of others to be seen by them. If you do, you will have no reward from your Father in heaven.

"So when you give to the needy, do not announce it with trumpets, as the hypocrites do in the synagogues and on the streets, to be honored by others. Truly I tell you, they have received their reward in full. But when you give to the needy, do not let your left hand know what your right hand is doing, so that your giving may be in secret. Then your Father, who sees what is done in secret, will reward you."

Now perhaps in most instances, your motives were pure. To an extent, I don't see this as always being a bad thing. Sometimes, people can be blinded by the issues they deal with privately.

Many of you right now are in a place that you know you love God, and honor Him with all your heart. Let me tell you—He's aware of your labor of love and sacrifice. And the tables are about to turn in your favor. When it's your time, it's your time! You will cross over!

★★★

WHAT TO LOOK FOR

Let me share with you nine things you can anticipate when you cross over.

1. Favor from unlikely places.
2. Clarity of thought (you will realize it was all necessary).
3. Preferential treatment wherever you go.
4. Your influence will expand.
5. God will give you supernatural stability.
6. You'll have a greater sense of discernment.
7. You can expect "make-up grace" on your behalf.
8. Covenant connections with character will come (not those who are critical of your every move).
9. You will build a greater depth of confidence that makes you unshakable in your faith.

When you recognize your gift and allow it to cultivate, it can open up opportunities for you to cross over into the blessings and promises of God.

Proverbs 18:16 NIV

A gift opens the way and ushers the giver into the presence of the great.

"Some of the best doors are not always open doors; they're doors that were closed, Selah."

The Lord will cause you to cross over and enlarge your territory, and you'll be able to enjoy the labor of it.

Deuteronomy 12:20 NIV

When the LORD your God has enlarged your territory as he promised you, and you crave meat and say, "I would like some meat," then you may eat as much of it as you want.

PROPHECY

Let me just take another moment here to prophesy the word of the Lord over your life,

For the time has come for Me to STAND STRONG in your life. Much has been lost and taken from you, but I declare, I am the God of RESTITUTION and RECOMPENSE. Just as I did with my servant Daniel when I came for his words, I will do even greater in thee. For the very solution to your dilemmas are coming now! I am a God of REPOSITIONING and RECKONING, continue to put Me first. The world is about to see My hand resting mightily upon thee, for now the time is to arise Zion, for the glory of the Lord is upon thee.

I decree that there shall be a coming forth of a REMNANT that I have declared will stand. A birthing and producing is about to occur in such a MASSIVE WAY. (I sense these words MASSIVE and MORE in such a strong way.)

I declare you will go FULL TERM and not abort this time! The

world and the church will begin to see that this is your year, without a doubt! The MASSIVE is coming! The Massive IS COMING! "For I am releasing a bold wind," says the Lord, "a wind that will cause your enemies to halt, and a wind that will advance you into victory. For even in the first quarter will I begin to release my Prophets, like unto the Prophet Gad, and the very holds over your life for years will snap and break!"

I hear things snapping and cords breaking in the spirit! This will not be a year of repeating lack and curses but of the new. "I am changing your current now to a new now! Get ready to soar, my sons and daughters. For there is a prophetic grace I'm releasing in this first portion of this year that will set the course for you throughout this year. The Gads are coming with the troops and the assistance of heaven. They're going to release words that break the HOLD! Prophets, get ready for an unusual grace to rest upon you like never before."

This will be the year, I declare, for many of you to break records in history, raise the bar, and establish your course of prosperity in the things of God! "I will release over your life as I did over my servant Moses, a grace for supernatural testimonies."

I declare that the anointing of ALL is about to bombard your life this year, and you will never be the same afterwards!

★ ★ ★

CONCLUDING REMARKS

In closing, I want to add this: When there is a point in your life that you have to cross over to the other side of something, there should always be a conviction to remain Focused and Full of Faith. Fellowship as often as you can with the Holy Spirit. Be very selective in who you identify as your friends and those with whom you share private information with.

And lastly, avoid the Fraud at all cost. Not everyone will share your enthusiasm and passion for what the Lord is doing in your life. Learn how to guard and govern the activity in your mind. It is crucial for your moving to the next place in life.

I'll just say it like this: If there is something that lingers or stands out in your mind, remember you are the interior decorator, and perhaps it's time to change the wallpaper in your mind. Our minds can get covered by so many things. For example, being in a comfort zone or just being stuck with fear.

"Your mind is so powerful, never forget this. It possesses the power to either conform or to create."

Let's continue to lean into our God-given assignments and continue in forward motion toward our destination.

Stay close to the ones who will release the wind into your sails and not the ones who will put holes in them. As I often say, "there are two types of people that come into your life: Those who will 'inspire' you and those who will 'expire' you." Discern the difference, and cross over to the other side… because better is waiting for your arrival.

I declare, a flood is coming. A flood is coming, and Pharaoh will be overthrown by the strong hand of the Lord. He will never see your face again and neither will you see his, because you're going to be hidden under the blood.

Be encouraged, for the cloud of the Lord will lead you by day and the pillar of fire from the Lord by night.

You're here now; let's cross over together. Let me take your hand because better is on the other side. Boom, Boom, Boom!!!

Nehemiah 2:11-18 MSG

"Come—Let's Build the Wall of Jerusalem"

And so I arrived in Jerusalem. After I had been there three days, I got up in the middle of the night, I and a few men who were with me. I hadn't told anyone what my God had put in my heart to do for Jerusalem. The only animal with us was the one I was riding.

Under cover of night I went past the Valley Gate toward the Dragon's Fountain to the Dung Gate looking over the walls of Jerusalem, which had been broken through and whose gates had been burned up. I then crossed to the Fountain Gate and headed for the King's Pool but there wasn't enough room for the donkey I was riding to get through. So I went up the valley in the dark continuing my inspection of the wall. I came back in through the Valley Gate. The local officials had no idea where I'd gone or what I was doing—I hadn't breathed a word to the Jews, priests, nobles, local officials, or anyone else who would be working on the job.

Then I gave them my report: "Face it: we're in a bad way here. Jerusalem is a wreck; its gates are burned up. Come—let's build the wall of Jerusalem and not live with this disgrace any longer." I told them how God was supporting me and how the king was backing me up.

They said, "We're with you. Let's get started." They rolled up their sleeves, ready for the good work.

I believe that the time has come for you to build something that's great, something that states you were once here, something that makes a mark that cannot be erased, and something that others will learn and benefit from.

"THE CONTINUATION"

7 WAYS TO MAXIMIZE EVERY MOMENT OF THE DAY THIS YEAR

Day 1: Be Respectful and Considerate

Consider doing a random act with no strings attached, whether honoring someone or blessing them.

Luke 6:30-36 KJV

Give to every man that asketh of thee; and of him that taketh away thy goods ask them not again. And as ye would that men should do to you, do ye also to them likewise. For if ye love them which love you, what thank have ye? For sinners also love those that love them. And if ye do good to them which do good to you, what thank have ye? For sinners also do even the same. And if ye lend to them of whom ye hope to receive, what thank have ye? For sinners also lend to sinners, to receive as much again. But love ye your enemies, and do good, and lend, hoping for nothing again; and your reward shall be great, and ye shall be the children of the Highest: for he is kind unto the unthankful and to the evil. Be ye therefore merciful, as your Father also is merciful.

Day 2: Be Confident

Don't be afraid to step out and be unique, because nothing just happens when you're stuck in timid territory.

Hebrews 10:35-36 NIV

So do not throw away your confidence; it will be richly rewarded. You need to persevere so that when you have done the will of God, you will receive what he has promised.

Day 3: Be Adventurous

Attempt to do something you've never done before. Distance yourself from the norm.

Numbers 13:30 NIV

Then Caleb silenced the people before Moses and said, "We should go up and take possession of the land, for we can certainly do it."

Day 4: Be Creative

Unleash what's been dormant on the inside of you.

Exodus 35:35 NIV

He has filled them with skill to do all kinds of work as engravers, designers, embroiderers in blue, purple and scarlet yarn and fine linen, and weavers—all of them skilled workers and designers.

Day 5: Be Independent

Take the initiative to implement and develop yourself.

Psalm 119:45 NIV

I will walk about in freedom, for I have sought out your precepts.

Day 6: Be a Dreamer

You'll never limit yourself if you continue to follow the pattern that was ignited on the inside of you by the Holy Spirit. Continue to remind yourself, write it down if need be. When you tap into the Holy Spirit, there is no limit as to what can unfold and be unleashed in your life.

Habakkuk 2:2-3 NIV

Write down the revelation and make it plain on tablets so that a herald may run with it.

For the revelation awaits an appointed time; it speaks of the end and will not prove false.

Though it linger, wait for it; it will certainly come and will not delay.

Day 7: Be Brave

Remember that the Greater One is always with you.

1 Chronicles 28:20 NIV

David also said to Solomon his son, "Be strong and courageous, and do the work. Do not be afraid or discouraged, for the Lord God, my God, is with you. He will not fail you or forsake you until all the work for the service of the temple of the Lord is finished."

52 DECLARATIONS THAT WILL DEFEAT BEING DORMANT

I want to end with this apostolic charge of 52 Declarations, and pray that they will build something you never thought possible. I urge you to do something that you've never attempted before that will redefine who you are, and refine your destiny.

★ ★ ★

I declare that this will be the year that I will cross over into a land flowing with wealth and supply.

I declare that Pharaoh will not follow me into my future, and his influence will be broken from my bloodline.

I declare that I am crossing over to better in every area of my life: in my choices, in my friends, in my business partnerships, in my ministry, and in my family.

I declare that my current "now" has just shifted to a new "now", which is the supernatural.

I declare that doors are about to open in a massive and major way for me and my family this year.

I declare that I am about to enter into the sweet spot of the supernatural, and nothing can stop me or block me.

I declare the very thing I've been working on for God in this season is about to explode.

I declare that I am standing right in the middle of my next miracle; and as I lean forward, I'll fall into favor.

I declare that optimum opportunities are about to be presented to me that will blow my mind.

I declare a "shabar" over the debt in my life (which in Hebrew means "a smashing to pieces").

I declare the earth will open up; and as it yields what belongs to me, all of my adversaries will be swallowed up in the grave.

I declare and call to attention every seed that I have sown. May the people who are supposed to bless and assist me remember me now.

I declare the doors that were once locked will now swing open for me.

I declare the strong hand of the Lord over all my affairs.

I declare the supply of heaven is now at my disposal.

I declare no one working witchcraft against me shall prosper, but it shall reverse back on them.

I declare that the yoke of lack will be broken off of my bloodline, and I'll never live that way again.

I declare that liabilities will decrease as my net worth increases.

I declare that every illegal door that I opened in the spirit realm is being sealed shut, in Jesus' name.

I declare that my mind will be daily regulated by the Word and not the world.

I declare that my thoughts are pure, my heart is pure, and my intentions are pure towards others.

I declare that I will grow in wisdom, as Jesus did in **Luke 2:52**.

I declare that I will become more focused than I've ever been in my entire life.

I declare that God will connect the right connections, and give me the boldness to let go of the wrong ones in my life.

I declare that everything will fall into place as it relates to my Kingdom assignment; from my branding, to my advertising, and even to others who will invest in my dream.

I declare that the grace of God is always abounding in every endeavor of my affairs.

I declare that I and my family will experience the goodness of the Lord.

I declare that only words of affirmation and confirmation will come from my mouth.

I declare that my body will forever choose to glorify God, in the church and in the marketplace.

I declare that this is my time to walk in the blessing of the Lord, and own it.

I declare I will not be affected by any setback; only encouraged to stay in the game.

I declare that I am the secret weapon of wealth for my family, my church, my job, and my bloodline; and nothing will convince me otherwise.

I declare that my seed has been selected and secured to become wealthy.

I declare that my mind will be alert and attentive to the Devil's tactics.

I declare that as long as there's breath in my body, I will proclaim His works in my life.

I declare that everything that was dead in my life will be resurrected now by the power of God, in Jesus' name.

I declare that which was hidden from me will be revealed.

I declare that resources and revenue will come from every direction in my life this year.

I declare that testimonies will become the daily norm for me.

I declare that I will author and produce a book that will be a best seller.

I declare that I will become a magnet for success and witty inventions will spring up out of my spirit.

I declare that favor will come upon my life as with Jabez **(1 Chronicles 4:10)**; and that all of my enterprises will increase and never be barren.

I declare that what God is about to do in my life will get the attention of the world.

I declare that excuses and procrastination will never exist in my life again.

I declare that my level of prayer, praise, and worship will draw me even closer to God.

I declare that every gate that was closed to my destiny, closed to my ministry, closed to my business, or closed to my marriage, will be opened again, in Jesus' name.

I declare that I am an arrow that will be shot forth in this hour to bless the nation.

I declare that I will have fruit in my life that will remain and never end.

I declare long life over my body and my bloodline. I am covered by the angels of the Lord, and goodness and mercy will accompany me.

I declare that my light will shine so brightly that it will cause others to come into the Kingdom and glorify God.

I declare that I will walk with the fire of the Lord, in the power of the Lord, and that wonders will manifest out of my life.

I declare that I will walk in dominion and authority and cause destruction to the Enemy's kingdom. God is raising me up to be a sower on a whole new level; and I will walk in obedience when it comes to sowing into the Kingdom.

Author Biography

"Many call him 'The Mailman' because of his on-point delivery of the Word of God. To others, he's an anointed vessel with a 'right now' word for a prepared people…"

D. John Coleman

Dr. D. John Coleman is declaring the Word of the Lord in a time he has labeled "the changing of the guards." He was called by God at the age of seventeen and was licensed and ordained at the age of nineteen under the Pentecostal Assemblies of the World (P.A.W.).

Dr. John has:

- an AA Degree in Business Management from Phillips College
- a Bachelor of Arts in Ministry with an Emphasis on Biblical Studies
- a Master of Arts in Christian Education
- a Doctor of Philosophy in Ministry from Midwest Christian College and Seminary

Dr. John has a mandate to bring a realization to the Body of Christ that it is God's desire for His people to establish a relationship with Him, instead of a "religion-ship." He is playing a pivotal role in reaching this generation and equipping them to activate the gifts within them. A cloud of testimonies including financial and healing miracles have manifested as a result of his ministry.

He has previously authored six books:
- Power Points to Prosperous Living
- The Chambers of Chenaniah – 12 Foundational Truths to Praise & Worship
- Spiritual Reflections – 52 Prophetic Tips to Prevent Prophetic Slips
- Worship Wisdom 4:24 - Reset My Worship
- Rising of the Thoroughbreds – A Guide to Finding Balance in Prophetic Ministry
- 55 Power Points to Building, Balancing, and Birthing Your Prophetic Gift

One point that he emphasizes is: "There are two types of people that come in your life: those that inspire you and those that expire you."

Along with his wife, Dr. John has spearheaded many community initiatives and outreach programs, which have raised tens of thousands of dollars to help families in need. Their effect and contributions in the communities they service are too numerous to mention. He has traveled and preached locally, nationally, and internationally; yet he is committed to his family, his global ministry (Kingdom Church International)—which he founded with his wife—and his local church, where he is the apostolic overseer. Empowered People Church is a non-denominational assembly which he also co-founded with his wife. Their vision is to "Empower God's People for Kingdom Living and Kingdom Advancement in the Earth."

Dr. John and his wife, Kisia, live in a suburb of Chicago and are the proud parents of five children: a son and daughter of their own, two orphaned nieces, and an orphaned nephew.

Author Contact Information:

Subscribe to our YouTube channel @ D. John Coleman Ministries

Facebook @ Deland John Coleman or Prophet D. John Coleman

Twitter @ Delandjcoleman

Instagram @ d.johncoleman2020

For bookings, contact - info@trykci.org

www.ingramcontent.com/pod-product-compliance
Lightning Source LLC
LaVergne TN
LVHW061046070526
838201LV00074B/5189